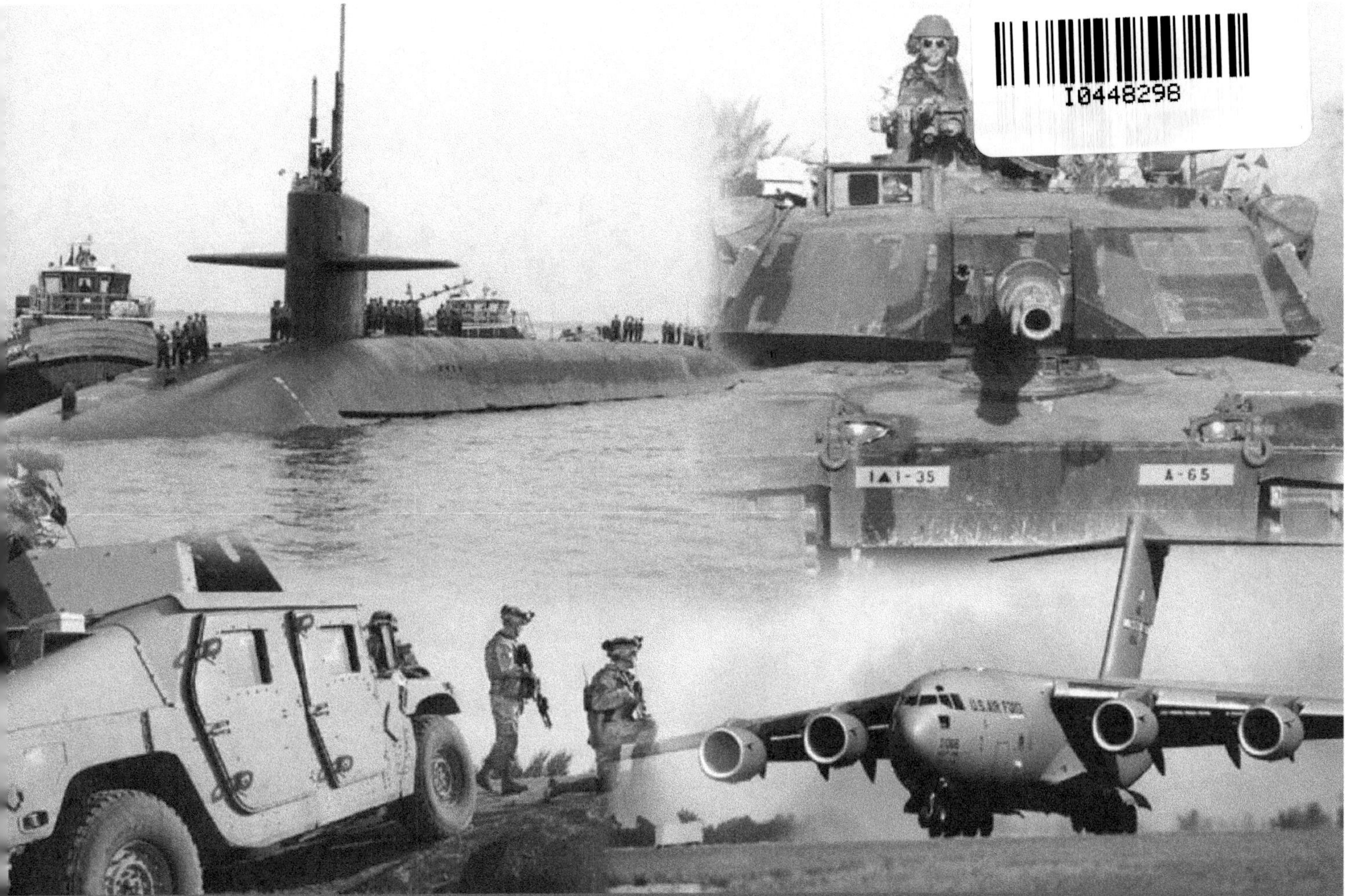

Defense Industrial Base Sector-Specific Plan

An Annex to the National Infrastructure Protection Plan

2010

U.S. Department of Defense

DEFENSE INDUSTRIAL BASE
CRITICAL INFRASTRUCTURE PROTECTION
SECTOR COORDINATING COUNCIL

May 2010

The Honorable Dr. Paul N. Stockton
Assistant Secretary for Homeland Defense and Americas' Security Affairs
2600 Defense Pentagon, Room 5D414
Washington, D.C. 20301-2600

Dear Secretary Stockton:

As Chairman of the Defense Industrial Base (DIB) Sector Coordinating Council (SCC), I hereby acknowledge your issuance of the DIB Sector-Specific Plan (SSP) in support of the National Infrastructure Protection Plan (NIPP). The DIB SCC member industry associations and companies appreciate the opportunity to contribute to strengthening resiliency within the DIB sector by participating in the development, refinement, and employment of the SSP.

The DIB SCC is encouraged by the progress made in nurturing the important public/private partnership codified within the NIPP and guided by the SSP. Our collaborative planning efforts continue to enhance the framework that enables DIB private sector CIKR owners and operators to engage in critical infrastructure protection value-added activities important for our nation's security.

On behalf of the DIB SCC, I acknowledge that we:

Earnestly support the critical infrastructure protection mission, vision, goals, and concepts, and will work with the Department of Defense and other sector partners to implement this Plan.

Have had the opportunity to provide insights and direction on the unique needs, concerns, and perspectives of DIB CIKR owners and operators.

Will continue to collaborate with designated DoD representatives exercising authority as the Sector-Specific Agency and other sector partners at all levels of government and private industry.

Will work with the Department of Defense, Department of Homeland Security, private sector CIKR owners/operators and others to improve physical, personal, cyber, and supply chain security; risk-based investment decision-making; and information sharing throughout the sector.

Sincerely,

Barry Bates

Major General, USA (ret)
DIB SCC Chairman

Preface

The Defense Industrial Base (DIB) is an unmatched element of national power that differentiates the United States from all potential opponents. In 2009, the Secretary of Homeland Security published the updated National Infrastructure Protection Plan (NIPP). The NIPP provides the overarching approach for the nation's critical infrastructure and key resources (CIKR) protection initiatives as a single integrated national effort. The Department of Defense (DoD) as the Sector-Specific Agency (SSA) for the DIB is responsible for leading the collaborative, coordinated effort to identify, assess, and improve the risk management of critical infrastructure across the DIB with its partners.

As Assistant Secretary of Defense for Homeland Defense and Americas' Security Affairs, I am pleased to publish our second edition of the DIB Sector-Specific Plan (SSP). The SSP outlines a common vision, goals, and approach in applying risk management activities to the sector. This plan is a product of extensive collaboration across DoD, its interagency partners, and representatives of the private sector, both national and international owners and operators that range from small proprietors to Fortune 500 corporations.

The 2010 DIB SSP reflects continued maturation of the relationship between government and private sector DIB partners. The extent and diversity of DIB relationships have produced the following positive results:

- Consensus-driven and logically constructed goals, objectives, implementation actions, and metrics;
- A coherent set of risk mitigation activities (RMAs) that is aligned with the 2009 NIPP framework and lays the roadmap for continued improvement of protection and resilience efforts throughout the sector;
- A more extensive understanding of cybersecurity issues, the importance of information as an asset itself, and the specifics of a focused RMA on cybersecurity;
- Evolving partnership mechanisms such as the organization of the Defense Security Information Exchange, Information Sharing Working Groups and the DoD DIB Cybersecurity/Information Assurance program to support private sector cybersecurity activities.

This plan is a living document that will evolve as the national security environment changes. To this end, the DIB partners are committed to work together to review the plan so that the resulting revisions reflect the highest level of preparedness and readiness for the risk mitigation activities that keep the DIB resilient. Protection of the DIB is paramount to maintain the competitive advantage in executing U.S. national strategy.

Paul N. Stockton

Assistant Secretary of Defense for Homeland Defense
and Americas' Security Affairs
U.S. Department of Defense

Todd M. Keil

Assistant Secretary for Infrastructure Protection
U.S. Department of Homeland Security

Table of Contents

List of Tables and Figures

Executive Summary

The President, in Homeland Security Presidential Directive 7 (HSPD-7),[1] designated the Department of Defense (DoD) as the Sector-Specific Agency (SSA) responsible for leading a collaborative, coordinated effort to identify, assess, and improve the risk management of critical infrastructure within the Defense Industrial Base (DIB). In HSPD-7, the President also directed DoD to produce the DIB Sector-Specific Plan (SSP) in collaboration with private sector and interagency partners. These HSPD-7 provisions are detailed in chapter 8. This DIB SSP outlines the DoD approach to executing its SSA responsibilities.

In response to HSPD-7 and in coordination with other SSAs, the Department of Homeland Security (DHS) developed the National Infrastructure Protection Plan (NIPP). The NIPP establishes a framework for a coordinated national effort to protect critical infrastructure that includes all levels of government, the private sector, academia, and international organizations and allies.

DoD collaborates with DHS and other SSAs and Federal agencies to ensure the DIB SSP is consistent with and fully supports national critical infrastructure and key resources (CIKR) protection and resilience efforts.

This 2010 DIB SSP reflects the maturation of the relationship between the government and private sector DIB partners. The increasing extent and diversity of DIB relationships produced the following positive results:

- Consensus-driven and logically constructed goals, objectives, implementation actions, and metrics;

- A coherent set of risk mitigation activities (RMAs) aligned with the 2009 NIPP framework;

- A more extensive understanding of cybersecurity issues, the importance of information as an asset itself, and the specifics of a focused RMA; and,

- Evolving partnership mechanisms such as organization of the Defense Security Information Exchange and Information Sharing Working Groups.

Continued growth is expected in all of the alliances between DoD, the defense and commercial industries, and all sector partners. The sector is embarking on an increased partnership-oriented approach to refine, develop, and carry out strategic plans and program implementation actions important to the protection and resilience of the sector. DoD, through the Government Coordinating Council (GCC) will assertively pursue the active engagement of its Sector Coordinating Council (SCC) counterparts and all sector partners to refine existing and develop new processes required to eliminate unacceptable levels of risk.

DoD developed many of the sector's risk management processes described in the SSP. This approach to developing a sector risk management process has proven to be insufficient for a variety of reasons. DoD plans to shift from this approach to one that

---

[1] Homeland Security Presidential Directive 7, Critical Infrastructure Identification, Prioritization, and Protection, December 17, 2003.

is all encompassing, inviting the diverse perspectives of the defense industry; other national sectors; Federal, State, tribal, and local governments; and other partners. Several steps will be taken to achieve greater collaboration and inclusiveness.

To increase collaboration and inclusiveness, the sector partners will jointly develop a 2010–2011 DIB Sector Business Plan. The business plan will guide sector partners in their pursuit of equal partnership. The Business Plan's foundation will include a joint examination of risk management processes and products including:

- Criticality determination and prioritization
- Vulnerability and risk assessment
- Information sharing
  - Criticality
  - Cybersecurity
  - Threat and warning
- Physical access control to DIB CIKR sites

In the pursuit of a more resilient defense industrial base, the SSA and DIB must address different, but closely related needs and issues. For example, each has different needs for threat and vulnerability information in this consumer-supplier equation. The processes that produce that information may also differ in their focus and detail. The SSA is committed to dedicate more time and resources in working with the DIB SCC to understand and address each other's respective needs and concerns. Particular emphasis will be devoted to the areas of cybersecurity information sharing, the insider threat, industrial espionage, and reengineering processes and practices to increase effectiveness while eliminating non-value added activities.

To ensure effective integration with the NIPP and conform to the SSP guidance, DoD and its DIB CIKR partners developed the DIB SSP that is summarized below.

Introduction

The DIB Sector is the worldwide industrial complex that enables research and development (R&D), as well as design, production, delivery, and maintenance of military weapons systems, subsystems, and components or parts, to meet U.S. military requirements. The DIB partnership consists of the DoD components and DIB companies which prioritize and coordinate protection of DIB CIKR.

The DIB partners make several planning assumptions, including that the fundamental purpose of the DIB is to provide products and services to support national defense and, that as the principal Federal customer and consumer of DIB products and services, DoD contracts with the global private sector DIB companies that it determines will best respond to its unique business and military needs.

Chapter 1: Sector Profile and Goals

The DIB Sector consists of government and private sector organizations that possess capabilities to support military operations directly; certain laboratories and capabilities to produce small-quantity, uniquely military materiel; and other specialized services that support military operations. The private sector component of the DIB consists of hundreds of thousands of independent and competing domestic and foreign companies, and supply chains delivering a vast array of products and services to support DoD business and military requirements.

The DIB Sector under the NIPP framework consists of several coordinating bodies, including the Critical Infrastructure Partnership Advisory Council (CIPAC), DIB GCC, and DIB SCC, each of which is a forum for DIB Sector partners to represent their interests and constituencies.

DoD (the DIB SSA) released the first version of the SSP in 2007. Since then, DoD and DIB CIKR owners/operators continue to build strong relationships based on mutual trust aimed at meaningful improvements to DIB protection and resilience. The partners continue to build new relationships and strengthen existing ones, build two-way information-sharing methods and techniques, and engage in frequent and ongoing dialogue on a diverse array of DIB CIKR issues.

DoD works with other Federal departments and agencies, foreign governments, and other international organizations to address DIB CIKR located outside the United States. DoD is developing an international strategy to improve protection and resilience of DIB assets, and to ensure the continued availability of CIKR outside the United States.

This SSP also provides an overview of the DIB partnership vision, as well as protection and resilience goals.

The DIB Sector vision is to collaboratively eliminate or mitigate unacceptable levels of risk to physical, human, and cyber infrastructures, thus ensuring that DoD continues to fulfill its mission and that DIB activities to support national security objectives, public health and safety, and public confidence are effective.

The DIB GCC and SCC developed a comprehensive set of interlocking goals, objectives, RMAs, implementation actions, and metrics. This SSP represents a complete revision of the goals and RMAs developed in 2007–2008. The DIB Sector defines five goals to achieve the DoD vision.

Goal 1—Sector Risk Management: Use an all-hazards approach to manage the risk-related dependency on critical DIB assets.

Goal 2—Collaboration, Information Sharing, and Training: Improve collaboration within a shared knowledge environment in the context of statutory, regulatory, proprietary, and other pertinent information-sharing constraints and guidance.

Goal 3—Personnel Security: Mitigate the risk created by personnel with unescorted physical or logical access to critical DIB assets in conformance with pertinent industry best practices, including regulatory and statutory requirements.

Goal 4—Physical Security: Manage the risk created by threats to and vulnerabilities of critical DIB physical assets.

Goal 5—Information Security (Cybersecurity/Information Assurance(CS/IA)): Manage risk to information that identifies or describes characteristics or capabilities of DIB CIKR, or that by its nature would represent a high risk/high impact to the CIKR or DIB asset.

Chapter 2: Identify Assets, Systems, and Networks

DoD identifies critical assets, systems, and networks using a process similar to private sector business impact analysis. High-consequence assets are identified based on the importance of missions and functions to the enterprise the asset supports, in this case DoD and its national defense mission.

The Defense Contract Management Agency (DCMA) is the DoD implementation agent for this program. DCMA solicits DIB critical assets nominations from DoD components based on its analysis of DoD missions, and from the DIB based on its knowledge of manufacturing and supply chain factors. DCMA then uses a set of screening criteria to determine the criticality of a nominated asset based on the impact to national defense mission if the asset were unavailable.

In 2010–2011, DCMA will lead collaborative efforts to continue mapping DIB CIKR owners/operators, assist the DIB GCC and DIB SCC record known dependency relationships for each DIB CIKR, augment data analysis with recognized infrastructure analysis experts, and collaborate across agencies. The DIB partnership will prioritize oil, natural gas, electricity, water, information technology, communications, and transportation infrastructure.

Other changes from the 2007 SSP include a continuous process for identification and greater involvement of DIB CIKR owners and operators in the process and development of an improved automated capability to facilitate nominating, identifying, and vetting.

DoD collects data from DIB Sector partners through questionnaires, public sources, and the examination of proprietary, nondisclosure, and purchasing agreements. DoD works through the Department of Commerce Bureau of Industry and Security to collect additional data using their data collection authorities. Also, DCMA collects pertinent data through voluntary onsite vulnerability assessments conducted by the National Guard. There are no regulations requiring DIB partners to submit infrastructure data to the SSA. DIB asset owners provide data on a voluntary basis with assurances that DoD uses appropriate measures and procedures to protect business-sensitive and proprietary information.

Since the 2007 SSP, DoD has become an accredited partner in the DHS Protected Critical Infrastructure Information (PCII) Program and follows strict requirements regarding use, handling, and protection of private sector proprietary and business-sensitive information. In addition to the activities described above, DCMA leverages its global contract management enterprise to acquire, validate, maintain, and protect fundamental industrial data and specific DIB asset data. Classified and the other most sensitive Defense Critical Infrastructure Program (DCIP) data or PCII resides in electronic product portfolios in DoD classified systems.

DoD periodically reviews all DIB CIKR data submissions for accuracy and currency, consulting with CIKR owners and operators to verify whether the data is correct. Because some DIB CIKR data is classified and many CIKR personnel do not hold security clearances, DoD works with DHS to facilitate the security clearance process for selected private sector CIKR personnel for the purposes of discussing, processing, and managing this essential information.

DoD classifies, stores, and disseminates data in accordance with the DCIP Security Classification Guide. Data classified up to SECRET is transmitted on the SIPRNET between DoD and cleared defense contractor companies that are DCIP participants with approved access. In addition, DoD is improving protection of sensitive unclassified DoD information residing on or transiting DIB unclassified networks under the DoD CS/IA program. This program has established the DIB Network (DIBNet) for cyber threat information sharing (classified up to SECRET and unclassified) between DoD and qualified DIB partners participating in the program.

Chapter 3: Assess Risks

The NIPP, based on criteria set forth in HSPD-7, provides that SSAs consider four categories of consequences: public health and safety impacts, economic impacts, psychological impacts, and impacts on governance and mission assurance. The category most relevant for the DIB is the impact on the national defense community's ability to execute its roles, responsibilities, and missions as assigned in statute and in Executive Orders, policy, and strategy. In addition, the DIB Sector must determine the impact of other infrastructure sectors on DIB operations.

There are no regulations requiring DIB companies to conduct risk assessments, but such requirements may be included in defense contracts. Many DIB companies conduct targeted risk assessments. Working within the DIB partnership, DoD aims to ensure awareness and use of risk assessment and management best practices throughout the DIB.

Risk assessment is a function of three factors: consequence, threat/hazard, and vulnerability.

- **Consequence:** The DoD asset, system, and network identification process described in chapter 2 determines whether a DIB asset warrants designation as CIKR. DoD identifies the consequence of asset loss to its missions early in the risk assessment process. The consequence assessment is independent of the cause for the loss.

- **Threat/Hazard:** DoD considers the full spectrum of threats and hazards to the DIB. The National Guard's Critical Infrastructure Protection (CIP)-Mission Assurance Assessment (CIP-MAA) team will continue to invite local law enforcement and counterintelligence personnel to DIB CIKR awareness briefings to foster a relationship with DIB CIKR management and staff. The DIB partnership will continue to draw on multiple sources of threat and hazard information. Examples are (1) the DHS fusion center for threat and hazard information—the Homeland Infrastructure Threat and Risk Analysis Center (HITRAC) and (2) the DoD-DIB Collaboration Information Sharing Environment (DCISE), which provides a threat information-sharing and reporting capability and is responsible for the fusion, analysis, production, and dissemination of cyber threat products.

  The most serious threat to the DIB is the cyber threat. This comes in many forms (e.g., insider threat, phishing). The biggest issue confronting the DIB is how information security is being implemented, i.e., system users not following procedures or system administrators not applying fixes to known vulnerabilities. The DIB relies on commercial-off-the-shelf (COTS) information system products that sometimes offer a host of vulnerabilities to those who would exploit them. The vulnerabilities are sometimes significant and other times too subtle to detect easily. In fact, these vulnerabilities are the subject of widespread exploitation efforts by individuals and groups within and outside the U.S. The purported reasons for these exploitation efforts range from altruism to espionage. The U.S. Government and the DIB must defend against this and other vulnerabilities regardless of the perpetrator's motivation. The U.S. Government and the DIB must implement a viable information security program with protection, detection, and response measures to thwart vulnerability exploitation. The timely detection of emerging cyber threats and the communication of these threats among the DIB partners is a vital part of this process.

- **Vulnerability:** The cornerstone of DIB CIKR vulnerability assessment is the CIP-MAA. A CIP-MAA considers an "on-the-ground" refinement of the impact (consequence of loss) and evaluates the exploitability of a wide range of possible vulnerabilities and risk vectors. The CIP-MAA also evaluates plausible threats/hazards whether from natural disaster, technological failure, human error, criminal activity, or terrorist attack. This approach ensures consideration of relevant factors for each DIB asset, as well as the relative prioritization of risks to DoD missions.

  Vulnerabilities are always specific for a particular DIB CIKR. However, DIB CIKR often share similar vulnerabilities in physical, personnel, and cyber security defenses. The number of DIB CIKR requiring a vulnerability assessment translates to a long lead time to complete CIP-MAAs for all DIB CIKR. The DIB SCC has therefore sponsored a risk screening capability to rank DIB CIKR to aid the process of scheduling CIP-MAAs based on relative importance and urgency to the sector.

The DIB CIKR risk assessment process evaluates these three factors to assess risk and determine the likelihood of direct, indirect, temporary, or permanent loss or degradation of production capacity or services that would adversely impact national defense missions.

Chapter 4: Prioritize Infrastructure

After DIB CIKR risks are assessed, prioritization considers the risks and weighs the effectiveness and timeliness of risk mitigation options, costs, and the time to restore a critical capability to an acceptable level of performance.

In the past three years, the DIB Sector has prioritized its CIKR annually through the Asset Prioritization Model. The model supports infrastructure prioritization by factoring in such data as policy and evolving DIB Sector risks. Recent improvements to the model streamline its operation and improve its validity. The improvements will enable prioritization modeling at any time, thus moving away from the annual snapshot.

Chapter 5: Develop and Implement Protective Programs

The composition of the DIB Sector continues to change with the ongoing consolidation and globalization of the defense industry. This fact, along with the number of Federal, State, and local authorities having situation-based roles in CIKR protection and resilience, complicates the responsibility landscape. To clarify this situation and help de-conflict possible gaps and overlaps in protection responsibilities, the DoD SSA established the following layered defense protection approach for DIB CIKR:

- DIB asset owners are responsible for the first level of protection.

- As the seriousness of a threat escalates, local civilian law enforcement authorities augment and reinforce the protective efforts of CIKR owners and operators.

- If the response from local authorities provides insufficient protection, local authorities may call upon State or Federal law enforcement to provide additional protection.

- In more serious situations, a State governor may request support under State Mutual Assistance Compacts, ask for Federal assistance, or employ the National Guard to enhance protection. If authorized by the President or Secretary of Defense, with the concurrence of the State Governor concerned, National Guard personnel could conduct this protective mission in title 32, section 502 (f) status.

- When warranted, the President may direct the use of U.S. military forces to protect threatened DIB CIKR assets.

The DIB partnership is goals-focused. The goal areas are sector risk management; collaboration, information sharing, and training; personnel security; physical security; and CS/IA. The DIB Sector partnership reviews its goals and risk mitigation activities at least annually to determine whether adjustments are necessary.

The DIB partners will develop and implement protective programs in response to DIB Sector goals and objectives. Protection and resilience programs apply at the individual DIB CIKR level. Because voluntary participation is part of the overall strategy, trust building and relationship development are key factors for DIB CIKR protection and resilience improvements. The DIB SSA and SCC partners facilitate trust and relationship development with DIB CIKR owners/operators through the governance structures established in the DIB SSP. Chapter 8 describes these structures.

The DIB SSA also collaborates in other relationships with other government agencies, the private sector, laboratories, and academia. This collaboration explores new concepts for protection and resilience, such as in relevant national and international standards, identifies "best practices" protection programs, coordinates Federal CIKR protection and resilience efforts, and determines DIB dependencies on other infrastructure sector services.

DoD and several members of the DIB Sector are implementing new collaborative mechanisms to support cybersecurity and information assurance. Particular emphasis in 2010–2011 will improve the protection of DoD information on unclassified DIB systems.

Specific prevention and protection needs and programs are subject to examination and acceptance by DoD and each DIB company. There are many options, such as:

- DIB partnership collaboration to examine the costs and benefits of additional protection measures;

- Awareness visits that include local law enforcement and first responders to strengthen relationships, security, and preparedness;

- DIB partnership collaboration to reduce risk from an attack or hazard by sharing best practices and tools to make risk mitigation easier;

- DIB partnership collaboration with CIKR owners and operators to determine the steps necessary to reduce risk, decide which additional measures will be instituted, and develop a strategy to allocate the costs associated with changes; and,

- DoD and DIB asset owners and operators may consider using the Defense Priorities and Allocations System (15 CFR Part 700) to expedite the timely delivery of industrial goods and services.

Chapter 6: Measure Progress

The DIB GCC and SCC are responsible for jointly developing, validating, and updating DIB Sector metrics to track SSP implementation progress. DoD records and reports DIB Sector metrics annually to DHS through the Sector Annual Report (SAR).

A primary progress indicator used to measure CIKR protection effectiveness is the number of successfully completed CIP-MAAs and awareness visits. In Fiscal Year (FY) 2009, DCMA and the National Guard Bureau conducted 30 awareness visits and 20 onsite assessments. From FY 2005 through FY 2009, a total of 144 awareness visits and 52 onsite assessments have been completed. The proposed schedule to meet the goal by 2013 will include conducting approximately 25–30 CIP-MAAs annually, with continued emphasis on dependency analysis.

In support of planned metrics reporting for the 2010 SAR, the DIB SSA, GCC, and SCC will develop an approach to deploy sector metrics. The sector will conduct six-month reviews of outcome metrics at CIPAC meetings and determine the extent to which DIB CIKR partners are achieving the intended DIB Sector outcomes.

The DIB Sector CIKR partners developed a set of metrics that pertain directly to implementation of the sector's protection and resilience goals. These metrics appear in the 2010 SAR. Chapter 6 contains 45 implementation actions and 67 outcome metrics directly supporting the goals presented in chapter 1.

Chapter 7: CIKR Protection Research and Development

The DIB recognizes that a fully operational R&D plan is instrumental for identification and development of technologies to identify threats, assess risk and vulnerability, and enhance the resilience and protective posture for the sector. Since 2007, DIB has been generating requirements, assessing the processes, and mapping the way forward toward development of an R&D plan for the sector. The SSA will collaborate internally with DoD agencies and collaborate with other SSAs and owners and operators to develop a focused DIB Sector program in the near term. This approach will enable identification of areas where R&D would be beneficial, identify and leverage initiatives currently underway, and champion new R&D initiatives that align with the sector.

DIB Sector R&D requirements are generated from information received from owners and operators and other sector partners, generally via the GCC/SCC, coupled with threat and risk information. To date, DIB Sector capability gaps have been submitted through the annual reporting process and are included in the DHS R&D Plan:

- Protection and Prevention – "Ensure interoperability with HSIN and DCIP COP"

- Insider Threat Detection

- Entry and Access Portals – "Facilities access and credentialing"

The DIB Sector plans to establish an ad hoc CIPAC DIB R&D Working Group with a mission to define and institutionalize the process for organizing and analyzing R&D and risk information, and reporting sector operational requirements and capability gaps to DHS.

To stimulate DIB Sector R&D activities, DoD will:

• Leverage the DHS R&D efforts and share those approaches with the DIB CIKR owners/operators and other CIKR partners;

• Identify DIB Sector technology requirements annually;

• Solicit an annual list of current CIP R&D initiatives from the White House Office of Science and Technology Policy to evaluate their potential support of DIB requirements; and,

• Compile its annual integrated list of technology requirements in support of DIB and submit them through the DHS capability gap statement template.

The DIB SCC will provide independent operational capability and technology gap information through the CIKR Cross-Sector Council that coordinates cross-sector initiatives.

Chapter 8: Managing and Coordinating SSA Responsibilities

Chapter 8 provides HSPD-7 citations of DIB SSA responsibilities and describes the management processes DoD uses to execute its responsibilities as the DIB SSA.

The chapter also describes information-sharing mechanisms, as well as the processes, programs, and tools the DIB Sector uses to protect the CIKR information it collects.

The DIB Sector has progressed in its relationships with CIKR partners since 2007. DoD will continue to build interpersonal and collaborative relationships with the CIKR owners/operators. Both the DIB GCC and SCC established working groups to discuss issues of significance. The councils, operating under CIPAC, will continue to refine information-sharing requirements and the characteristics of unwanted events, consequences and impacts of loss, and vulnerabilities that if exploited could result in the degradation or loss of an asset.

Processes and Responsibilities

DoD reviews the SSP annually with its DIB GCC and SCC partners, making revisions as required by the program and to align with DHS guidance. The Assistant Secretary of Defense (ASD) for Homeland Defense and Americas' Security Affairs (ASD (HD&ASA)) leads DIB SSP reviews and updates to the SSP with full participation of the DIB GCC and SCC. Each member signs a letter attesting to its role in reviewing and implementing the DIB SSP.

DoD collaborates with its DIB Sector CIKR partners to acquire the information necessary to prepare the SAR.

DoD has maintained centralized responsibility for building, managing, and tracking the DIB CIP program budget and resources. ASD (HD&ASA) uses a strategic and performance management model to meet both internal DoD CIP and DIB SSA responsibilities. DoD reviews the DIB mission and vision statements, guiding principles, and organizational values annually, and refines and prioritizes the goals presented in chapter 1 in collaboration with sector partners.

In the near term, ASD (HD&ASA) will continue to manage the policy, oversight, and advocacy elements of the budget, and DCMA will manage the integration and coordination elements to execute SSA executive agent responsibilities. The DIB GCC and SCC will contribute to the development of sector requirements and priorities to inform the resource management process.

DoD understands that a successful DIB risk management effort requires effective training, education, and outreach. DoD seeks to enhance those efforts and support DIB Sector CIKR partners in expanding their education and training programs and initiatives. To communicate the importance of these efforts effectively, DoD will meet with senior executives and managers, intelligence analysts, assessment teams, and security personnel from DoD, DHS, and the National Guard Teams who conduct assessments.

Implementing the Sector Partnership Model

The DIB GCC and SCC are the principal coordinating bodies for the DIB Sector. These bodies are the sector's representatives to the Government Cross-Sector Council and CIKR Cross-Sector Council, respectively, and serve as the DIB leadership focal points for national level coordination. In addition to the DIB GCC and SCC, the following are examples of high-profile participants in the sector partnership model:

- CIPAC is a Federal Advisory Committee Act–exempt body (established pursuant to 6 U.S.C. 451) that enables industry and government partners to discuss DIB-related CIP issues, normally in the form of joint GCC and SCC meetings.

- The Homeland Infrastructure Foundation-Level Database (HIFLD) Working Group promotes domestic and international infrastructure geospatial information sharing, protection, and knowledge management. HIFLD is a coalition of Federal, State, and local government agencies that collaborate with Federally Funded Research & Development Centers and private sector partners.

- The State, Local, Tribal, and Territorial Government Coordinating Council provides liaison representatives who are influential and knowledgeable leaders on CIKR-related issues at the State, local, tribal, and territorial levels to the DIB GCC.

- The North American Technology and Industrial Base Organization (NATIBO) facilitates technology and industrial base efforts between the United States and Canada in support of North American security.

Information Sharing and Reporting

DoD has identified the venues and mechanisms for sharing information with the various DIB CIP communities of interest. These communities include: domestic organizations (including industry); international private industry; international coalitions and allies; Federal, State, and local governments and agencies; and other DoD organizations.

The most significant challenge for the DoD partnership is to establish relationships with the private sector such that the sector trusts the government to protect its business-sensitive, proprietary, and confidential information from public disclosure and misuse. As a first step in establishing that trust, DoD became an accredited partner in the PCII Program.

DoD will continue to classify information in accordance with applicable regulations and ensure that classified information remains in appropriately accredited channels.

DoD will continue to develop information-sharing policy, processes, and procedures to enhance two-way communication between DoD and DIB asset owners, building on the success of the DoD DIB CS/IA pilot program and the establishment of the DIB GCC and SCC.

Introduction

The Defense Industrial Base (DIB) Sector is the worldwide industrial complex that enables research and development (R&D), as well as design, production, delivery, and maintenance of military weapons systems, subsystems, and components or parts, to meet U.S. military requirements. The DIB partnership consists of the Department of Defense (DoD) components and DIB companies that prioritize and coordinate protection and resilience of DIB critical infrastructure and key resources (CIKR).

Homeland Security Presidential Directive 7 (HSPD-7) designated DoD as the Sector-Specific Agency (SSA) responsible for leading a collaborative, coordinated effort to identify, assess, and improve risk management of critical infrastructure within DIB. HSPD-7 also directed DoD to produce the DIB Sector-Specific Plan (SSP) in collaboration with private sector and interagency partners. In addition, the National Infrastructure Protection Plan (NIPP) establishes a framework for a coordinated national effort to protect critical infrastructure that includes all levels of government, the private sector, academia, and international organizations and allies.

The DIB SSP has taken on a more partnership-oriented approach to describe the status of DIB protection efforts, and outlines the sector vision, goals, objectives, risk assessment methodology, and comprehensive plan to implement tactical-level processes that lead to improved protection and resilience of DIB assets. The DIB SSA will continue to pursue engagement of its Sector Coordinating Council (SCC) counterpart and all DIB partners to ensure an encompassing approach to eliminate gaps affecting sector operations and allow diverse perspectives from other sectors and State, local, and tribal governments to strengthen DIB sector resilience. Protection of DIB CIKR depends on efforts to protect and/or make resilient, functions associated with other critical infrastructure sectors, such as Energy, Information Technology, Communications, Critical Manufacturing, Chemical, and Transportation Systems.

The DIB Sector's vision is that its partnership engages in collaborative risk management activities to eliminate or mitigate unacceptable levels of risk to physical, human, and cyber infrastructures, systems, and networks, thus ensuring that DoD continues to fulfill its mission. DIB activities support national security objectives, public health and safety, and public confidence.

The following assumptions underpin the DIB SSP:

- The fundamental purpose of the DIB is to provide products and services to support national defense.
- DoD is the single SSA authority responsible for coordinating U.S. government DIB protection and resilience programs.
- As the principal Federal customer and consumer of DIB products and services, DoD contracts with the global private sector DIB members that it determines will best satisfy its business and military requirements.
- DIB members participate in national protection and resilience programs willingly and on a voluntary basis except in those instances where regulatory or contractual authority exists between DoD and a DIB private sector entity. DoD has no authority to compel an entity to comply with non-regulatory or non-contractual needs, requests, or demands.

- DIB partners continue to pursue common goals and perspectives on approaches to mitigate risk to CIKR. They will jointly refine their objectives as the relationship matures.

- The DIB SSP assumes an all-hazards environment, with a particular emphasis on the threat of cyber attacks against DoD which will continue to increase in frequency and sophistication.

The DIB SSP structure conforms to the NIPP risk management framework and the intent of the Department of Homeland Security (DHS) SSP guidance summarized as follows:

- **Set Sector Goals:** Define specific outcomes, conditions, end states, or performance targets that collectively constitute an effective protective and resilience posture.

- **Identify Infrastructure:** Develop an inventory of the assets, systems, and networks, and the critical functions they provide, including infrastructure located outside the United States, that make up the nation's critical infrastructure, and collect information pertinent to risk management.

- **Assess Risks:** Determine risk by combining potential direct and indirect consequences of a terrorist attack or other hazard and known vulnerabilities to various potential hazards, with general or specific threat information.

- **Prioritize:** Aggregate and analyze assessment results to determine asset, system, and network criticality, and present a comprehensive picture of national infrastructure risk to establish priorities and provide the basis for protection and resilience planning and informed allocation of resources.

- **Implement Protective Programs and Resilience Strategies:** Select appropriate protective actions or programs to reduce the risk identified and secure the resources needed to address priorities.

- **Measure Effectiveness:** Use metrics and other evaluation procedures at the national and sector levels to measure progress and assess the effectiveness of national and sector level CIKR protection programs.

- **CIKR R&D:** dentify and describe R&D requirements, processes, programs, and initiatives that are relevant to improving the protection and resilience of DIB, per DHS SSP guidance.

- **Managing and Coordinating DIB SSA Responsibilities:** The Secretary of Defense designated the Assistant Secretary of Defense (ASD) for Homeland Defense and Americas' Security Affairs (HD&ASA) as the coordination focal point for the various elements of DoD in executing its full range of SSA responsibilities. This includes collaboration with all relevant governmental agencies and the private sector; conducting or facilitating vulnerability assessments of the DIB Sector; and developing and implementing risk management strategies to mitigate all-hazards risk to DIB CIKR.

The DIB partnership faces several challenges in implementing this SSP. Among these are:

- **Voluntary Participation.** Private sector participation in implementing the NIPP is voluntary. Many large defense industry firms place great emphasis on protecting their physical, human, and cyber infrastructure, while many more small and medium-sized businesses are challenged to allocate the capital required to participate in this national endeavor. In addition, DoD and DIB have a dominant consumer/supplier relationship versus the regulatory relationship common to some of the other SSAs and their respective infrastructure sectors.

- **Interdependencies.** Identifying, understanding, and addressing the impact of commercial interdependencies. The DIB partnership has not addressed commercial infrastructure interdependencies in a systematic way.

- **Information Sharing.** Meaningful and timely information sharing is too often obstructed. Classified DCIP-related information is not being shared with cleared DIB partners. Private sector proprietary information received by DoD creates information-sharing barriers. Further, the absence of private sector critical asset information sharing with the SCC adversely impacts sector resilience.

- **Shared End State.** Overcoming the lack of shared understanding and accepted standards in areas such as cybersecurity for unclassified information systems, personnel screening, and physical security, especially at the subcontractor and supplier level, is critical.

Subsequent SSP sections address these challenges.

This revision of the DIB SSP reflects a great deal of maturation in the relationship of the government and private sector partners. The increasing extent and diversity of DIB relationships produced the following positive results:

- Consensus-driven and logically constructed goals, objectives, implementation actions, and metrics (chapters 1, 5, and 6);

- A coherent set of risk mitigation activities (RMAs) aligned with the 2009 NIPP framework (chapter 5);

- A more extensive understanding of cybersecurity issues and a common lexicon for cyber infrastructures, the importance of information as an asset itself, and the specifics of a focused RMA (chapter 5, appendix 4); and,

- Evolving partnership mechanisms, such as the organization of the Defense Security Information Exchange, Information Sharing Working Group, and the DoD DIB Cybersecurity/Information Assurance (CS/IA) program (chapters 1, 2, and 3).

The common theme underpinning SSP changes is the increased understanding among all DIB partners about the sector's characteristics, purpose, capabilities, and the limitations of a voluntary public-private partnership.

1. Sector Profile and Goals

This chapter describes the nature and complexity of the DIB Sector and current state of relationships among sector partners. It also presents the DIB partnership's vision and protection and resilience goals. Since publication of the 2007 DIB SSP, DoD has made progress and continues to foster activities with DIB CIKR owners and operators to build strong relationships based on mutual trust in the pursuit of meaningful improvement to DIB protection and resilience. The DIB has responded very positively and supports DIB Sector efforts. Partners continue to build new and strengthen existing relationships, build two-way information-sharing methods and techniques, and continue frequent and ongoing dialogue across the diverse array of DIB partnership challenges.

1.1 Sector Profile

The DIB Sector consists of government and private sector organizations that can support military operations directly; perform R&D; design, manufacture, and integrate systems; and maintain depots and service military weapon systems, subsystems, components, subcomponents, or parts—all of which are intended to satisfy U.S. military national defense requirements.

The government component of the DIB consists of certain laboratories, special-purpose manufacturing facilities, capabilities for production of uniquely military materiel such as arsenals and ammunition plants, and other services.

The private sector component of the DIB consists of hundreds of thousands of independent, competing domestic and foreign companies and supply chains, delivering a vast array of products and services to DoD. DIB defense-related products and services equip, inform, mobilize, deploy, and sustain U.S. military and allied military forces worldwide. The DIB companies also deliver national security products and services to other Federal agencies.

The DIB taxonomy consists of segments and sub-segments that produce and maintain weapon system platforms, components, and expendables. DoD uses the taxonomy detailed in table 1-1 to characterize the DIB Sector and help determine CIKR criticality. This characterization primarily applies to impact analysis for DoD mission accomplishment, but also contributes to public health and safety, economic, continuity of government, and public confidence impact analysis.

1.2 CIKR Partners

The DIB Sector consists of a complex set of interpersonal relationships and several important coordinating bodies. The DIB GCC, DIB SCC, and CIPAC each provide a forum where DIB partners can represent their interests and constituencies. The descriptions of each group below illustrate the diverse roles and missions of DIB partners and the collaborative mechanisms developed by them to continue mature collaboration.

Table 1-1: DIB Segments, Sub-segments, and Commodities

Industry Segments			
Industry Segments	Industry Sub-segment	Industry Segments	Industry Sub-segment
Aircraft	Fixed Wing	Munitions	Missile Tactical
	Rotary Wing		Missile Strategic
	Unmanned Aerial Systems		Missile Air/Air
Ships	Surface		Missile Air/Surface
	Sub-Surface		Missile Defense
	Unmanned Underwater Vehicles		Missile Surface/Air
Tracked and Wheeled Land Vehicles	Combat Vehicles		Missile Surface/Surface
	Tactical Vehicles		Precision Guided Munitions
	Unmanned Ground Vehicles		Ammunition
Electronics	Electronic Warfare		Missile Defense Agency
	Command, Control, Communications, Computer and Intelligence (C4I)	Space	Launch Vehicles
			Satellite
	Avionics		Missile Defense Agency
Soldier Systems	Chemical Biological Defense Systems	Mechanical	Transmissions (Air/Auto)
	Clothing and Textiles		Propulsion (Diesel/Rocket/Turbine)
	Subsistence/Medical		
Structural	Castings/Forgings		Hydraulics
	Composites		Bearings
	Armor (Ceramic/Plating)		Nuclear Components (includes Depleted Uranium)
	Precious Metals		

1.2.1 Government Coordinating Council

DoD and DHS co-chair the DIB GCC and thus play a key role in fulfilling HSPD-7 SSA collaboration.

The DIB GCC is the public sector forum that facilitates member engagement for collaborative discussions on sector policy issues. These issues include cybersecurity; integration with State, local, tribal, and territorial jurisdictions; and GCC infrastructure interdependencies.

The objectives highlighted in the DIB GCC's charter mirror this and charge the council members to coordinate across all CIKR sectors. The DIB GCC membership includes representatives of the Departments of Defense, State, Treasury, Justice, and Commerce, with support provided by agency personnel. The GCC amended the charter in 2009 to include members of the State, Local, Tribal, and Territorial Government Coordinating Council (SLTTGCC), enabling better integration of DIB Sector equities at all levels of government.

1.2.2 Sector Coordinating Council

The DIB SCC presents the principle face of the defense industry to DoD for collaboration on DIB protection and resilience issues. Since its formation under the leadership of the National Defense Industrial Association in July 2007, the SCC has continued to help mature the public-private partnership within the DIB.

The DIB SCC consists of representatives of several defense-related professional associations:

- National Defense Industrial Association (NDIA);
- Aerospace Industries Association (AIA);
- National Classification Management Society (NCMS);
- American Society of Industrial Security (ASIS) International;
- Industrial Security Working Group (ISWG); and
- Defense Security Information Exchange (DSIE).

DIB SCC members exchange relevant information freely to identify issues and potential solutions of mutual concern to the defense industry and the government. To further this effort, the SCC chartered four standing committees to address issues of major importance to the DIB:

- **Information Sharing** to develop a trusted information-sharing environment wherein appropriate information can flow seamlessly between DIB industry associations, CIKR owners and operators, and sector partners to improve sector security and resilience through reduced risk for DIB CIKR.
- **Risk Management** to facilitate effective risk management processes across the DIB private sector, including DIB CIKR owners and operators and representing a cross-section of all risk management equities of the DIB SCC enterprise.
- **Personnel and Physical Security** to collaborate with DIB CIKR owners and operators and other sector partners in developing a reliable capability to assess and maintain an acceptable level of human and physical asset risk, and to improve sector resilience through reduced risk to the sector's CIKR.
- **Information/Cybersecurity** to leverage trusted relationships to share information on cyber-related attacks, enable DIB industry partners to quickly alert others of any incident, and facilitate development and implementation of mitigation strategies supporting information assurance and asset protection of CIKR within the sector.

The DIB SCC meets regularly with representatives of the DIB SSA and GCC to continue to develop new protocols for sharing and protecting information about DIB CIKR.

The DIB SCC's Cyber Sub-council, DSIE, has been engaged in an outreach program to share cyber threat information across multiple sectors. This outreach program, sponsored by the National Security Telecommunications Advisory Committee (NSTAC), has developed into a pilot program called the Joint Collaboration Center (JCC). The JCC initially engaged the Financial

Sector Information Sharing and Analysis Center (ISAC), Information Technology (IT) ISAC, and Communications ISAC. The ultimate goal is to engage all 18 sectors as a component of the new National Cybersecurity and Communications Integration Center. In addition, the DSIE has signed an agreement with the United Kingdom's Aerospace and Defence Manufacturer's Information Exchange, extending information sharing internationally as well as across sectors.

1.2.3 Joint DIB CIPAC Information Sharing Working Group

Information sharing is the most significant challenge recognized by the DIB SCC and GCC. The DIB CIPAC Information Sharing Working Group (ISWG) began meeting in August 2009 to pursue the following objectives:

- Develop an information-sharing environment built on trusted relationships that facilitates two-way sharing that flows seamlessly among members to achieve improved protection and resilience;

- Identify broad categories of information to be shared;

- Define DoD requirements for timely information sharing with CIKR partners; as an example, the information-sharing group reviewed a variety of unwanted events—cyber insider threats, technology transfer, and manmade disasters/continuity of operations;

- Define, validate, and prioritize government and industry information-sharing requirements;

- Develop a DIB Sector Information Sharing Plan;

- Describe and facilitate resolution of information-sharing barriers and gaps; and,

- Highlight the need for enhanced information sharing throughout the sector.

1.2.4 Other Government Authorities

DoD collaborates with DHS which is responsible for the NIPP and other Federal agencies to ensure the DIB SSP is consistent with and fully supports national CIKR protection and resilience efforts. These Federal entities include:

- DHS, Office of Infrastructure Protection (IP);

- DHS, Office of Cybersecurity and Communications (CSC);

- Department of Justice, Federal Bureau of Investigation (FBI);

- Department of Energy (DOE);

- Department of Commerce (DOC);

- Department of the Treasury;

- Department of State (DOS);

- Office of Director of National Intelligence (ODNI); and,

- White House Office of Science and Technology Policy (OSTP).

Appendix 5 describes the DIB GCC roles of these organizations in detail.

1.2.5 International Organizations and Foreign Countries

DoD works with other Federal departments and agencies, foreign governments, and international organizations to address concerns relative to critical DIB/CIKR assets located outside the United States. DoD is developing an international strategy to improve protection and resilience of DIB assets and to assure the continued availability of CIKR outside the United States. DoD seeks to leverage the expertise of international partners to improve its own capabilities in counterterrorism, maritime interception, and other missions critical to an active, layered defense. Appendix 5 describes international relationships in more detail. Some of the key partnerships include:

- North American Technology and Industrial Base Organization Steering Group;
- Canadian Department of National Defense/U.S. DoD DIB Working Group;
- FBI legal attachés;
- U.S. DOS;
- North Atlantic Treaty Organization Defense Against Terrorism Program of Work CIP;
- Combatant Commands (COCOM) CIP officers;
- DoD DIB CS/IA – international pilot
- DHS/DoD–hosted International Critical Infrastructure Protection (ICIP) Working Group

Some DIB SCC member companies own and operate CIKR sites located outside the United States. Other facilities are foreign-owned. The DIB SCC will play an important role in advising and coordinating the DIB international strategy by assisting in identifying CIKR sites, performing self-assessments, building preparedness plans, and implementing risk mitigation actions as required.

1.3 Sector Goals, Objectives, and Risk Mitigation Activities

DIB Sector Vision Statement

The DIB Sector partnership engages in collaborative risk management activities to eliminate or mitigate unacceptable levels of risk to physical, human, and cyber infrastructure, systems, and networks, thus ensuring the Department of Defense continues to fulfill its mission. DIB activities support national security objectives, public health and safety, and public confidence.

The DIB GCC and SCC developed a comprehensive set of interlocking goals, objectives, RMAs, implementation actions, and metrics. This SSP represents a complete revision of the goals, objectives, and RMAs developed in 2007–2008. In support of the 2009 NIPP, the DIB partnership aligned implementation actions to a set of RMAs that now represent a roadmap to improve the overall protection and resilience of the DIB in 2010–2011. The relationship of RMAs to DIB Sector goals is illustrated in table 1-2.

Goal 1 – Sector Risk Management: Use an all-hazards approach to manage the risk-related dependency on critical DIB assets.

Objective 1A	As the SSA, DoD will identify and maintain an inventory of DIB assets.
Objective 1B	Conduct mission assurance risk assessments on DIB critical assets.
Objective 1C	SSA and DIB owners and operators apply risk management strategies to mitigate identified risks.
Objective 1D	Identify and manage the risk associated with dependencies (supply chain, dependent infrastructure assets, power, water, foreign suppliers) potentially impacting critical DIB assets.
Objective 1E	Improve the effectiveness of government threat reporting to officials, owners and operators responsible for critical DIB assets, local law enforcement officials, and other first responders.

Goal 2 – Collaboration, Information Sharing, and Training: Improve collaboration in a shared knowledge environment in the context of statutory, regulatory, proprietary, and other pertinent information-sharing constraints and guidance.

Objective 2A	Maximize participation of all DIB partners in a shared knowledge environment.
Objective 2B	Develop specific security awareness training and education for DIB partners.
Objective 2C	Share and advance sound risk management practices, including infrastructure asset resilience, mitigation of risks, and redundancy throughout the DIB.

Goal 3 – Personnel Security: Mitigate the risk created by personnel with unescorted physical or logical access to critical DIB assets in conformance with pertinent industry best practices, including regulatory and statutory requirements.

Objective 3A	Establish screening guidance and practices for un-cleared personnel.
Objective 3B	Mitigate insider threat through education and observation.

Goal 4 – Physical Security: Manage the risk created by threats to and vulnerabilities of critical DIB physical assets.

Objective 4A	Conduct baseline assessments on DIB critical assets.
Objective 4B	Determine response options available to reduce risk at all DIB critical facilities.
Objective 4C	Execute risk response.

Goal 5 – Information Security (Cybersecurity/Information Assurance): Manage risk to information that identifies or describes characteristics or capabilities of DIB CIKR, or that by its nature would represent a high risk/high impact to the CIKR or DIB asset.

Objective 5A	Protect information concerning critical DIB assets commensurate with the sensitivity of that information. Protection means any action to mitigate a threat that might result in exposure, injury, destruction, modification, subversion, manipulation, corruption, incapacitation, or exploitation of the information.
Objective 5B	Protect the DIB critical electronic information and communication systems, networks, and critical unclassified Information associated with critical defense acquisition programs and control systems and their interconnecting links to other sectors from damage, loss, corruption, or unauthorized access.

Chapter 5 lists 16 RMAs that DIB Sector partners collaboratively developed to achieve these five goals.

Table 1-2: Relationship of Goals to RMAs

	Goal 1 – Sector Risk Management	Goal 2 – Collaboration, Information Sharing, and Training	Goal 3 – Personnel Security	Goal 4 – Physical Security	Goal 5 – Information Security (CS/IA)
RMA 1 – Business Continuity Plans	X				
RMA 2 – CIKR Asset Identification and Prioritization	X				
RMA 3 – DCIP Resilience Guide and "Best Practices"		X		X	
RMA 4 – Dependency Analysis	X				
RMA 5 – DIB Local Asset Information Sharing	X			X	
RMA 6 – DIB Cybersecurity, Assurance, and Protection					X
RMA 7 – DIB Sector Outreach Activities		X			
RMA 8 – Exercise Programs	X				
RMA 9 – Incident Reporting and Response Information Sharing	X				
RMA 10 – Information Sharing Requirements Generation		X			
RMA 11 – Insider Threat Guidance and Application			X		
RMA 12 – Local Security Awareness Training		X			
RMA 13 – Mission Assurance Assessments and Followup	X			X	
RMA 14 – Personnel Screening Guidance and Application			X		
RMA 15 – Risk Response Planning and Implementation	X			X	
RMA 16 – Self-Assessment Tool	X			X	

1.4 Value Proposition

A consensus-driven partnership draws on the active, voluntary, and full engagement of all partners. DIB Sector partners realize the value proposition when all participants recognize the business value of their respective participation. Each value proposition listed below relates to one or more RMAs that are detailed in chapter 5.

The government gains value from the partnership in the following ways:

- Understanding DIB CIKR assets, systems, networks, facilities, and other capabilities (RMA 2, RMA 7, RMA 8, RMA 10);

- Identifying DIB CIKR dependency on other national infrastructure sectors (RMA 4, RMA 5, RMA 10, RMA 13);

- Increasing the ability to take action to reduce risk and respond to and recover from incidents (RMA 1, RMA 3, RMA 8, RMA 9, RMA 10);

- Applying industry best practices to address DIB CIKR security challenges (RMA 3, RMA 8);

- Increasing public-private problem definition and problem-solving collaboration (RMA 2, RMA 5, RMA 7, RMA 10); and,

- Developing robust relationships that are useful for sharing and protecting sensitive information on threats, vulnerabilities, countermeasures, and best practices (RMA 5, RMA 6, RMA 7, RMA 9, RMA 13).

Industry gains value from the partnership in the following ways:

- Aligning corporate and government planning and investments through a shared policy development and risk analysis framework (RMA 2, RMA 3, RMA 6);

- Expanding information sharing regarding specific threats and hazards, enabled in part by issuance of security clearances to private sector partners and resolution of security classification issues (RMA 3, RMA 7, RMA 10, RMA 11, RMA 14);

- Leveraging preparedness guidelines and self-assessment tools to manage risks more effectively and efficiently, corporation-wide down to the individual facility level (RMA 4, RMA 6, RMA 11, RMA 14, RMA 16);

- Targeting application of limited resources to the highest risk issues (RMA 4, RMA 8, RMA 12, RMA 13);

- Coordinating all-hazards planning across multiple agencies for assets and facilities considered to be at the greatest risk (RMA 4, RMA 6, RMA 7);

- Participating in joint R&D, modeling, simulation, and analysis programs (RMA 4);

- Leveraging national-level and cross-sector training and exercise programs as well as the National Incident Management System (RMA 3, RMA 5, RMA 6, RMA 8, RMA 10);

- Increasing access and input into cross-sector interdependency analyses (RMA 4, RMA 5, RMA 6);

- Establishing information networks among private sector partners and between the private sector and various Federal agencies (RMA 6); and,

- Identifying potential improvements in regulations (RMA 6).

2. Identify Assets, Systems, and Networks

This chapter describes the processes the DIB Sector uses to identify assets, systems, and networks, and to collect data pertinent to CIKR risk management. It also describes the roles and responsibilities of the various DIB partners in this process, and the procedures for protecting the sensitive and classified information that guides DIB Sector decisionmaking and risk management.

Since publication of the 2007 DIB SSP, the DIB Sector has scrutinized its CIKR identification processes and initiated adjustments to improve the quality of asset identification activities. DoD has refined the DIB identification criteria, streamlined the nomination and vetting process, and begun incremental development and implementation of electronic tools to expedite the identification process and collect supporting information. The DIB partnership has worked to comprehensively identify critical sector assets. In the coming years, the DIB Sector partners will fully develop and exploit these initiatives to identify CIKR with greater efficiency, while seeking opportunities for further improvement.

2.1 Asset Identification

DoD identifies critical assets, systems, and networks using a process similar to private sector business impact analysis. COCOMs thoroughly analyze documented mission-essential tasks (METs) for each assigned mission to determine the facilities, materiel, and services that are critical for executing each MET. Many of these critical assets are part of the DIB; others fall within the purview of other sectors. A structured mission analysis concurrently identifies critical assets and the consequence of their loss to the mission, thus allowing a priority focus and eliminating the necessity to catalog every possible DoD or DIB and private sector asset.

For the purpose of this document, the term, "cyber asset" is not used. Instead, DIB CIKR language will address cyber elements, components, and other infrastructure relative to identified DIB assets (facilities).

Cyber Highlights

The DIB SSA and the DoD DIB CS/IA program will work together to leverage existing DIB cyber capabilities and processes in support of DIB cyber resilience and protection of unclassified DoD information on DIB unclassified systems and networks. In addition, DSIE shares cyber information among the DIB partners in near real time to mitigate cyber attacks.

The Defense Contract Management Agency (DCMA) augments COCOM mission analysis by soliciting nominations for DIB critical assets. This additional process ensures a comprehensive examination of possible DIB CIKR.

To identify critical asset nominations, DCMA uses the following screening criteria that focus on impact to national defense missions:

- Single source, sole source, or defense-unique suppliers;
- Suppliers of products that have dual-use qualities;
- Suppliers of products that are used in multiple DoD programs;
- Suppliers with high requalification cost or long lead requalification timeframes; and,
- Suppliers developing and possessing advanced or emerging technology.

The criticality screening process focuses on each industrial facility. However, cyber infrastructure at facilities is not considered.

Since publication of the 2007 DIB SSP, the following major steps have been taken to identify and update the inventory of DIB CIKR:

- DCMA and DIB members identified potential suppliers meeting screening criteria.
- The Military Departments, DCMA, and other Defense Agencies have validated and updated the list of potential DIB CIKR.
- DCMA has coordinated the DIB Critical Asset List (CAL) with Military Department acquisition executives and Defense Agency directors.
- DCMA has submitted the DIB CAL to Deputy Undersecretary of Defense (DUSD) for Industrial Policy and then to Undersecretary of Defense (USD) for Acquisition, Technology, and Logistics (AT&L) for approval.
- The ASD (HD&ASA) have notified DIB CIKR owners/operators of their criticality designation.
- The ASD (HD&ASA) has submitted the DIB CAL and Important Capabilities List (ICL) to DHS.

DoD works with DHS and the other SSAs to identify overlaps and gaps in responsibility for DIB assets. The DIB SSA interacts with its partners under a flexible approach based on relevant circumstances. The DIB SCC recently requested establishment of a GCC/SCC CIPAC "ad hoc" working group to address DIB criticality issues. At the request of the SCC, the DIB partnership will enter into a process to more fully involve private sector partners in the identification and prioritization process, with the goal of publishing a jointly agreed process by December 31, 2010.

DoD maintains basic data on all DIB partners. This data provides a general characterization of potential critical assets, systems, and networks:

- Contractor and government entity code, name of company, street address, city, State
- Prime contractor or subcontractor
- Products, functions, production rates
- Critical technologies

- Contractor subject matter expert, facility security officers, and their contact information
- Programs, components, and subsystems
- Business overview (e.g., privately or publicly held, non-U.S. owned)

- Critical subcontractors (first and second tier), selection criteria, products, and services
- Sales, employment, capacity utilization, square footage
- Financial information

2.2 DIB CIKR Dependencies/Interdependencies

DIB owners/operators will collaborate to identify DIB Sector and cross-sector dependencies and interdependencies through the following actions:

- DIB CIKR owners and operators will embark on a joint public/private effort to develop a standard data call process for collecting private sector dependency/interdependency information.

- DIB GCC and SCC members will work to identify additional external dependencies/interdependencies through collaboration with other organizations that possess expert analytical capabilities, such as the Mission Assurance Division in Dahlgren, VA, and the CIKR Cross-Sector Council's Interdependencies Sub-council.

- DIB partners will work with other sectors, through the Partnership for Critical Infrastructure Security (PCIS) Interdependency Working Group and other mechanisms, to better understand and develop solutions to mitigate risks associated with critical dependencies/interdependencies and supply chain linkages. The priority focus will be on the Oil and Natural Gas, Electricity, Water, IT, Communications, and Transportation Systems Sectors and Subsectors.

The DIB partnership must consider three fundamental dependency relationships as it determines cyber risk.

- **Owned cyber infrastructure within a DIB facility:** Any vulnerability or threat to a cyber infrastructure is assessed as a single point of service that could become a single point of failure.

- **Owned cyber infrastructure outside the DIB facility:** Any vulnerability to a cyber infrastructure is considered a dependency that could become a single point of failure. If the cyber infrastructure were a communications or digital network, the dependency would be a DIB dependency on an IT or Communications Sector asset.

- **Corporate cyber infrastructure outside the DIB facility:** Any vulnerability to a cyber infrastructure is considered an inter- or intra-dependency, based on the sector where the element resides.

Cyber dependency information is collected on DIB CIKR as it becomes available during CIP-MAAs and is included in the CIP-MAA report to the DIB CIKR owner or operator. Additional dependency information may be provided by companies conducting self-assessments.

2.3 2010–2011 Initiatives in Asset Identification

- **Asset Identification Criteria and Process:** DoD, as the primary customer of DIB products and services, identifies the assets of importance to its operations and coordinates this perspective with other DIB Sector partners. The DIB SCC has suggested that incorporating the unique perspectives of DIB owners/operators might improve this process. Cleared CIKR owners often depend on sub tier suppliers, and therefore it might be useful to query them for nominations from essential sub tier suppliers to be considered for criticality screening. The GCC and SCC members will continue to review options to integrate these perspectives into the identification process for DIB critical assets.

- **DIB CIKR Assets Mapping:** DCMA will continue to work with the Joint Staff, COCOMs, and the military departments to map DIB assets to DoD missions. The DIB SSA has the responsibility to lead this comprehensive analytical effort.

- **Continuing DIB CIKR Asset Identification:** Identification, nomination, vetting, and approval of DIB CIKR will change from an annual process to an ongoing, continuous process beginning in FY 2010. In this new approach, employing jointly developed selection criteria and prioritization procedures, the ASD (HD&ASA), DCMA, and private sector owners and operators as represented in the SCC will analyze and vet all sites and facilities for designation or criticality, and actively engage with the owners and operators of those sites and facilities designated as critical. In addition, the USD (AT&L) will continue to approve an annual snapshot of DIB critical assets in accordance with DHS data call guidance. Chapter 5, RMA 2 describes specific implementation actions associated with this initiative.

- **Accelerated DIB CIKR Identification:** The DIB SSA will develop a semi-automated process to facilitate CIKR identification, nomination, and vetting to replace the existing complex process. The new process should significantly reduce processing times across the dispersed stakeholders. Chapter 5, RMA 2 describes specific implementation actions associated with this initiative.

2.4 Collecting Infrastructure Information

In addition to site surveys and visits, DoD collects business and industrial data from DIB Sector partners using questionnaires, public sources (e.g., Dun & Bradstreet), and examination of proprietary, nondisclosure, and purchasing agreements. DoD also cooperates with DOC's Bureau of Industry and Security (BIS) to initiate targeted data collection from specific defense-related industries and critical technologies using DOC/BIS's mandatory data collection authorities. DCMA collects additional pertinent data through CIP-MAAs, conducted by National Guard personnel.

To earn the trust of the private sector in receiving and protecting CIKR data, DoD became an accredited partner in the DHS Protected Critical Infrastructure Information (PCII) Program. DoD follows strict PCII requirements for the use, handling, and protection of private sector proprietary and business-sensitive information. The PCII Program offers protections from public disclosure for qualifying information voluntarily submitted by private industry. Many DIB CIKR owners and operators submit business-sensitive information under the program. DoD personnel are thoroughly trained in all PCII use, handling, and protection requirements prior to obtaining access to the information.

There are no regulatory requirements to provide infrastructure data among DIB partners. DIB asset owners provide data on a voluntary basis with assurances that DoD employs appropriate measures and procedures to protect business-sensitive and proprietary information.

In addition to the activities described above, DCMA leverages its global contract management enterprise to acquire, validate, maintain, and protect fundamental industrial data and specific DIB asset data. Tools, networks, and associated policy documentation are currently under development and implementation to facilitate these data collection and retention processes. The DIB SSA must reduce the burden in compliance with the Paperwork Reduction Act by collecting core information through the Office of Management and Budget–approved DD form 2737.

The most sensitive information resides in electronic product portfolios on a DoD classified system portal. This repository contains summaries of supporting information on DIB CIKR. The ASD (HD&ASA) and other DoD decision makers use this information for risk management and continuity of operations purposes. Information in the portfolio includes:

- General Information
- Industrial, Technology Capability, and Financial/Economic Assessments
- Industrial Base Studies
- Awareness Visit Reports and Follow-ups

- Sector Characterization
- Vulnerability Assessment Results and Follow-up Visits
- Continuity Plans
- Threat Assessments
- Other Assessment Results

- Self-Assessments
- Antiterrorism/Force Protection Education and Training Material
- Site Risk Assessments
- Asset-Supplied Briefings

2.5 Verifying Infrastructure Information

DoD periodically reviews all DIB CIKR data submissions for accuracy and currency, consulting with owners and operators to verify the data as required. When information is incomplete or inaccurate, DCMA collects additional information during follow-up site visits or telephone interviews with responsible DIB owners and operators.

The exchange of CIP-related information with elements of the private sector presents unique challenges in the DIB Sector. CIP information relative to a specific CIKR is classified, and many CIKR personnel do not hold security clearances. DoD works with DHS to facilitate the security clearance to process for selected private sector CIKR personnel for the purposes of discussing, processing, and managing this essential information.

Some DIB CIKR data is classified. DoD classifies, stores, and disseminates data in accordance with the Defense Critical Infrastructure Program (DCIP) Security Classification Guide. DoD classifies some DIB information up to the SECRET level. That information is transmitted within DoD via the SIPRnet. In the case of the DoD DIB CS/IA program, information classified up to SECRET is transmitted between DoD and cleared defense contractor (CDC) companies that are DIB program participants with approved access to the DIBNet. The DIBNet is a special-purpose network established for this capability.

2.6 Cyber Infrastructure

DoD is partnering with qualified DIB CDC companies through the DoD DIB CS/IA program. This partnership is improving the protection of sensitive, unclassified DoD information residing on or transiting private sector DIB unclassified networks. The program is expanding to include additional qualified CDCs using the DIBNet.

The DoD DIB CS/IA program conducts risk assessment and mitigation activities through its DoD DIB Collaboration Information Sharing Environment (DCISE) and DoD cyber intrusion damage assessments. Non-attributed findings and protective actions are incorporated into a range of program documents and disseminated to qualified CDC companies, as well as Government stakeholders.

Cyber Highlights

The focus of the DoD DIB CS/IA program is unclassified DIB systems and networks where sensitive DoD information resides or transits. The program is implementing the direction of the Deputy Secretary of Defense to "stop the bleeding."

The DSIE program involves DIB partners that share information on cyber attacks through use of an unclassified DHS secure portal. Such sharing enables the DIB to identify and share attack attributes quickly so that DIB partners can immediately apply mitigation techniques to stop the attacks. All information sharing is done in a multidirectional, networked, nonattributional method according to the NIPP and HSPD-7. This sharing now includes international participation through a partnership with the United Kingdom's Aerospace and Defence Manufacturers' Information Exchange (ADMIE). In addition, DSIE represents the DIB SCC in the cross-sector JCC pilot program. The DIB GCC and SCC are considering how to improve information sharing between the GCC and SCC and will continue to collaborate on solutions to address cyber threats. To this end a proposal has been submitted by the SCC to the GCC for consideration of the DSIE partnering with a component of DoD under CIPAC. If adopted, a multidirectional, networked, trusted information-sharing environment can be established. The DSIE has been invited to join the FBI and U.S. Secret Service in information sharing as well.

3. Assess Risk

Since publication of the 2007 DIB SSP, DCMA, as the Defense Sector Lead for the DIB Sector, has solidified its risk assessment approach based on a comprehensive mission decomposition of each CIKR. In addition, the sector updated the DIB assessment methodology and benchmark standards, established a framework for understanding threats relative to individual assets and regional clusters, and implemented lessons learned based on vulnerability assessments and after-action reviews. Over the next few years, the sector partners plan to incrementally incorporate cyber vulnerability and risk assessments into the risk management program.

This chapter describes the DIB risk assessment approach to ensure sector protection and resilience, including:

(1) Cross-sector protection efforts, coordinated with DHS, other Federal SSAs, State/local governments, and private sector entities;

(2) DIB Sector protection efforts coordinated by DoD, other Federal agencies, and industry associations; and,

(3) Asset, system, or network-specific protection efforts coordinated by DIB member companies.

Comprehensive risk assessment and subsequent risk management decisions are derived from applicable threat profiles and their likelihood of occurrence, along with associated vulnerabilities and consequential impact. While certain strategic-level threat scenarios may be well understood and applicable to the sector at large, the variability of threat scenarios, vulnerabilities, and impact consequences drives risk assessment activities to individual CIKR assets. With the accumulation of data resulting from such assessments throughout the sector, conclusions and observations regarding strategic-level threat information, dependency analysis, preparedness trends, and best practices will be understood and shared with stakeholders, particularly with asset owners and operators across the sector. Some of these best practices are discussed in the 2010 SAR.

3.1 Use of Risk Assessment in the Sector

The NIPP, based on criteria set forth in HSPD-7, guides SSAs to consider four categories of consequences: public health and safety, economic, psychological, and the impact on mission assurance. The last category is most relevant for the DIB as it relates to the impact on DoD's ability to execute its roles, responsibilities, and missions under the Constitution and as assigned in statute and Executive Orders, policy, and national and defense strategies.

There are currently no regulatory requirements for DIB companies to conduct risk assessments, although such requirements may be included in defense contract vehicles. In 2010, the DoD issued DoD instruction (DoDI) 5205.13 and a DoD Directive (DoDD) 5505.13E. Both address CS/IA and cyber incident reporting by DIB partners participating in the voluntary DoD DIB CS/IA pilot program. In addition, the program provides a DIB CS/IA Capabilities Benchmark and Questionnaire for program participants to conduct a self assessment. A proposed Defense Federal Acquisition Regulation (DFARS) clause on safeguarding and cyber incident reporting is currently under development. Major defense contractors routinely conduct targeted risk assessments as part of their business models. Working within the DIB partnership, DoD aims to ensure awareness and use of risk assessment and management best practices throughout the DIB.

DoD executes a mature, structured program aimed at assessing and mitigating risk in the DIB Sector. DoD accomplishes this through the DIB partnership and by working directly with appropriate DIB CIKR officials. As described previously, the program focuses on risk to DoD missions resulting from disruption or degradation of DIB CIKR. DoD continues to evaluate whether its practices and procedures are adequate to accommodate the broader focus and emphasis of the NIPP on criteria other than government capability/mission assurance to respond to national requirements. Based on longstanding experience, the DIB SSA expects that the potential DIB impact on public health and safety will not rise to the level of national significance.

DIB economic impacts are closely linked to an ability to provide government services. The DIB SSA postulates the potential adverse impact on the national economy from an isolated DIB disruption or failure to be insignificant. DIB Sector partners participate in the annual DHS-led national risk assessment process that focuses on improved capability to analyze additional economic, public health and safety, and public confidence factors. This process will facilitate recognition of changing conditions that could lead to incorporation of this information into future DIB risk prioritization considerations.

3.2 Screening Infrastructure

DoD, in collaboration with other DIB Sector partners, performs a screening of all candidate DIB critical assets based on the potential consequences of loss or disruption to DoD missions. DoD determines consequence of loss for DoD-owned assets as part of the overall mission decomposition. If the impact of loss results in mission failure, the asset is deemed critical regardless of how likely that loss might be. Clearly, potential threats, hazards, and exploitable vulnerabilities do not determine the criticality of an asset. Loss of DoD mission capability places the national defense at risk regardless of the reason for the lost capability, hence the dominance of this screening criteria in the DIB Sector risk assessment. This criterion also reflects the importance of the DoD-DIB consumer-supplier relationship in achieving overall mission assurance.

3.3 Assessing Consequences

CIKR provide products or services, or enable the provisioning of products or services, that respond to DoD mission requirements. Dependency analysis—the analysis required to identify and screen for CIKR—supports consequence assessment. The DIB partners determine the impact of CIKR loss or degraded performance in qualitative and quantitative terms. Qualitative consequence assessment includes specific narrative descriptions of reduced or eliminated military capability as a result of the CIKR being unavailable. A quantitative consequence assessment expresses the impact of CIKR loss or degraded performance with numbers. Examples include time or monetary metrics such as the maximum acceptable period of time the CIKR can be unavailable before there is a negative mission impact, or monetary loss of provisioning capability or capacity. Consequence assessments are independent of the reason for CIKR being unavailable; the cause for CIKR loss or performance degradation does not influence a consequence assessment.

When a DIB asset is determined to be a DIB CIKR asset, DCMA collects the following information:

- Buildings or other structures where industry manufactures or stores critical items

- Continuity and redundancy, including backups built into the asset (alternative sources of supply and backup production facilities)

- Existing protective actions (e.g., fencing, biometrics, firewalls)

- Dependencies a sector's asset has on other assets in the same sector, and dependencies between assets from different sectors

- Impact on sector in cases of loss or failure (e.g., economic, public health and welfare, public psyche, national security)

- Clearance levels and associated information

- Exposure to known foreign intelligence threats, such as treaty compliance regimes

- Dependencies (services and support an asset requires to function)

- Longitude and latitude

3.4 Assessing Vulnerabilities

DCMA completes DIB CIKR prioritization based on the consequence of loss before conducting asset-specific vulnerability assessments. This ensures that the highest consequence CIKR receives a vulnerability assessment first, and facilitates necessary mitigation activities as soon as possible.

The cornerstone of the DIB CIKR vulnerability assessment process is the CIP-MAA. Based on the prioritization of CIKR, DCMA will coordinate a schedule with CIKR owners and operators for CIP-MAAs that are conducted by the National Guard (for CIKR in the United States).

A CIP-MAA considers an "on-the-ground" refinement of the impact (consequence of loss) and evaluates the exploitability of a wide range of vulnerabilities and risk vectors. The CIP-MAA also evaluates plausible threats/hazards whether from natural disaster, technological failure, human error, criminal activity, or terrorist attack. This approach ensures consideration of relevant factors for each DIB asset as well as the relative prioritization of risks to DoD missions. Through FY2009 the SSA has completed comprehensive vulnerability assessments at 52 critical DIB asset sites. Aggregate analysis is currently underway to identify trends in risk profiles, dependencies, lessons learned, and best practices across the sector. The SSA plans to refine this analysis and incorporate future assessment results to share findings with industry and government stakeholders going forward.

Each CIP-MAA follows the same general process:

- The DIB CIKR site agrees to host a CIP-MAA.

- A State National Guard team is selected based on workload and CIKR site preferences, to lead the CIP-MAA.

- DCMA and DIB CIKR site legal counsel negotiate a memorandum of agreement (MOA) documenting CIP-MAA rules of engagement. The National Guard team requests a dependency data package from the appropriate government centralized analytical capability, typically the Dahlgren Mission Assurance Directorate or U.S. Army Corps of Engineers. This request provides for additional subject matter expert participation in the CIP-MAA, representing industry sectors such as transportation, power, water, and telecommunications depending on the assessment requirements for the particular DIB CIKR site.

- DIB CIKR owner/operator representatives are briefed thoroughly on what to expect from the CIP-MAA.

- An advance visit to the DIB CIKR site permits the assessment team to become familiar with the facility and to begin to develop a trusted relationship with facility management and staff.

- The assessment team develops a preliminary view of security issues and potential single points of service/failure.

- The assessment team conducts the assessment, which includes identifying factors such as the longest acceptable production delay without mission impact, and single points of service (potential vulnerabilities) and dependencies that could become single points of failure. The longest acceptable production delay factor is a key resilience criterion.

- The assessment team completes its assessment and conducts a classified out-brief for the cleared DIB CIKR official(s).

- The assessment team prepares a classified CIP-MAA report, retaining a copy and providing a copy to the cleared DIB CIKR official.

- After one year, DCMA conducts a follow-up visit with the DIB CIKR official to review risk management decisions, accomplishments, and vulnerability remediation/mitigation.

Other types of assessments include DHS Enhanced Critical Infrastructure Protection visits conducted by a Protective Security Advisor and sometimes coordinated with DoD, and self-assessments conducted by owners and operators. The DIB SCC's Risk Management Committee will develop a self-assessment tool that, when completed for a facility, will give a numeric value that represents risk in terms of the physical security posture of the facility. If constructed properly, the numeric value should decrease when vulnerabilities are adequately addressed. An eventual goal will be to jointly determine with the DIB SSA an acceptable level of risk. This tool will eventually have different modules to assess physical, cyber, and resilience risk. The SCC will begin with the physical security module in the third quarter of 2010 and continue during 2011.

Due to the complexity of international laws and engagement regulations, all international assets must be addressed on a case-by-case basis. Appropriate coordination with DOS, the appropriate Geographic Combatant Command, and the applicable host nation's government agency is necessary at all times. The DIB SSA must first engage through the appropriate interagency and foreign government channels before establishing a consensus-driven partnership with any overseas DIB asset.

DoD will continue to provide infrastructure protection awareness training to DIB CIKR owners and operators and facility personnel. The training also educates DIB personnel about their importance within the overall DoD mission requirements and acquisition process. The training focuses on:

- Protection of DoD interests;

- Protection of Federal interests;

- Mission assurance to the war fighter; and,

- Importance of fostering relationships with local responders and Federal, State, and local law enforcement/civil authorities for business recovery planning.

The awareness training also informs asset owners and operators of the protections applied to proprietary and business-sensitive information provided voluntarily to DoD, and gives an overview of DoD information-sharing responsibilities and procedures regarding vulnerability data.

In addition, the DoD DIB CS/IA program office and DCMA are taking steps to share best practices and build on natural synergies in support of the common goal of improving the resilience of the DIB, with a focus on cybersecurity. For example, the DIB CS/IA Capabilities Benchmark, based largely on the National Institute of Standards and Technology's 800-53 guidance, will be available as an optional tool to assist DIB Sector CIKR in improving cybersecurity situational awareness and their cyber postures.

DoD and CIKR owners/operators are adopting a multi-tiered approach to risk assessment. This approach begins with the current awareness training program as discussed above. DIB asset owners and operators are encouraged to evaluate their risk management practices consistent with DoD risk management principles. In collaboration with sector partners, DoD is developing self-assessment tools and programs that will be made available to DIB companies.

DoD projects further progress in this area during the present planning timeframe as DIB Sector partners continue to employ self-assessment processes and metrics on a voluntary basis. The 2009 DIB SAR describes these projects as key elements of the DIB Sector goals, objectives, RMAs, and metrics.

3.5 Assessing Threats

DoD will continue to consider the full spectrum of threats and hazards to the DIB in its risk assessment processes. The National Guard CIP-MAA team will continue to invite local law enforcement and counterintelligence personnel to DIB CIKR awareness briefings to foster a relationship with CIKR management and staff. In addition, with the concurrence of the DIB CIKR official, the assessment team will invite local law enforcement and emergency management personnel to participate in assessments.

DoD also continues to work closely with DHS to share CIKR-related threat and hazard information. The DHS Office of Intelligence and Analysis incorporates intelligence and other information from multiple sources to identify and assess threats. The Departments also share selected baseline infrastructure asset information, including the status of infrastructure services and anomalous activities. The close relationship with DHS will continue to ensure integration of information from the U.S. Coast Guard (USCG), Transportation Security Administration (TSA), Immigration and Customs Enforcement, Customs and Border Protection, and other vital threat information sources.

DHS maintains a fusion center for threat and hazard information, the Homeland Infrastructure Threat and Risk Analysis Center (HITRAC). HITRAC also maintains situational awareness of infrastructure sectors and works with the SSA and other Federal, State, local, tribal, and private sector partners to develop strategic assessments of risks by integrating threat information with information regarding unique vulnerabilities and potential consequences of each sector.

The most serious threat to the DIB is the cyber threat. The DIB relies on commercial-off-the-shelf (COTS) information system products that are often flawed in their design and implementation, thus offering a host of vulnerabilities to those who would exploit them. The vulnerabilities are sometimes significant and other times too subtle to detect easily. In fact, these vulnerabilities are the subject of widespread exploitation efforts by individuals and groups within and outside the U.S.

The DoD DIB CS/IA program focus is on protecting critical unclassified DoD information on unclassified non-DoD DIB systems and networks, a priority established when the program was initiated in accordance with Deputy Secretary of Defense direction to "stop the bleeding." This priority and urgency is because the threat from adversaries illegally exploiting and ex-filtrating DoD's current and future war fighting capabilities from DIB networks poses an unacceptable risk.

The DoD-DIB Collaborative Information Sharing Environment (DCISE), under the direction of the DoD Cyber Crime Center, provides a capability for threat information sharing and reporting, and is responsible for the fusion, analysis, production, and dissemination of cyber threat products. Since its operations began in February 2008, DCISE has provided intelligence-based cyber threat analysis and products to participants in the DoD DIB CS/IA program, while collecting, analyzing, and disseminating no attribution-based cyber incident report information from the program participants. The unique government-industry collaboration can serve as a model for other national-sector cyber threat information-sharing initiatives.

DSIE is a sub-council of the DIB SCC. The DSIE involves more than 30 DIB contractors and their cybersecurity employees who are responsible for protecting corporate networks. These companies and their employees have agreed to share information through a mutual non-disclosure agreement (NDA) between the companies and individual members. DSIE has also partnered with ADMIE for the same level of sharing. Whenever a member discovers new cyber information, the information is shared with all partners through the U.S. Computer Emergency Readiness Team (US-CERT) portal. This portal is managed by DSIE and its members for non attributional sharing in near real time. DSIE has also acted as the cyber strategic arm of the DIB SCC by representing DSIE in other DHS and DOJ cross-sector initiatives, such as the NSTAC JCC and the Cross-Sector Cyber Security Working Group (CSCSWG).

DoD, in coordination with the Office of the Director of National Intelligence (ODNI), will capitalize on appropriate defense and national intelligence assets to develop, support, and sustain an assessment of threats to DIB. The National Military Command Center (NMCC), Defense Joint Intelligence Operations Center (DJIOC), and associated Combatant Command Joint Intelligence Operations Centers, will coordinate with DHS watch centers, including US-CERT, the National Operations Center, National Infrastructure Coordination Center, and National Communications Center, to maintain awareness of and respond to all threats to the DIB. Furthermore, DoD, through NMCC and DJIOC, will work with other standing and ad hoc watch centers, such as those established by the FBI, DOJ, and Secret Service during National Special Security Events. The DJIOC coordinates the use of DoD assets and will work through ODNI to task national intelligence assets.

3.6 Assessing Risk

The risk assessment process for DIB CIKR provides an evaluation of factors that might cause direct, indirect, temporary, or permanent loss or degradation of production capacity or services that would adversely impact national defense missions. The evaluation includes:

- Industrial and business analysis that defines the business, economic, technology and production risks that might adversely affect the capability of the supplier to provide the critical material or service.

- Common commercial infrastructure analysis that maps critical supplier dependencies on the supporting commercial infrastructure sources such as energy, telecommunications, and transportation. These analyses identify potential single or significant points of failure, a reasonable range of remediation actions, and a suggested resolution action, where viable, to the appropriate Federal SSA.

- Vulnerability assessments that define supplier vulnerabilities, identify impact if lost, propose and rank countermeasures, and include CIP-MAAs and vulnerability self-assessments for use by DIB facility management and the government. This includes a self-assessment process for early identification, evaluation, and resolution of issues having a high impact on mission assurance.

- Threat assessments for the full spectrum of threats and hazards, including manmade actions taken by nation-states, national and transnational criminal entities, terrorist activities, accidents, and acts of nature.

4. Prioritize Infrastructure

This chapter describes the risk-based process for prioritizing DIB assets, systems, and networks. For the past three years, the DIB Sector has prioritized its CIKR annually through the Asset Prioritization Model (APM). Recently, the Argonne National Laboratory reviewed the APM and recommended improvements that DCMA implemented to streamline the model and improve its validity. The APM operates in a database environment to increase capacity, reduce entry requirements, and enable customized reports.

DIB CIKR partners seek to invest in assessment and remediation activities in the most effective manner possible. The SSA will plan to further engage the DIB SCC in the asset identification and prioritization process. To that end, DoD, in collaboration with other DIB Sector partners, prioritizes DIB CIKR based on the potential DoD mission impact, as previously described. This prioritization considers the national defense missions and the consequence of DIB CIKR degradation or loss, exploitable vulnerabilities, threats and hazards, risk mitigation options and costs, and the time to restore a critical capability to an acceptable level of performance.

4.1 Asset Prioritization Model

The DIB SSA prioritizes DIB CIKR using the APM. The APM assists analysts in understanding the DIB Sector more clearly and in allocating resources more wisely. DCMA will implement a refined and independently validated version of the APM in FY 2010. DoD will use the APM to prioritize DIB CIKR for both analysis and reduction of risk, and to prioritize assets for additional assessment and vulnerability mitigation investment based on their relative criticality. For FY11, DCMA will work with the DoD DIB CS/IA program office (Assistant Secretary of Defense for Networks and Information Integration/DoD Chief Information Officer (ASD (NII)/DoD CIO)) as well as with other government stakeholders, to consider cyber risk and the APM.

4.2 Asset Prioritization Factors

The APM provides a score using five major factors and 24 sub factors. Figure 4-1 illustrates the factors and their respective weighting. All the factors are given a score of 1 through 5 (1 being least critical, 5 being most critical). Each factor score is assigned a percentage weight ranging from 10 to 35. The sum of the individual weighted scores establishes an overall score between 0 and 100.

4.3 Asset Prioritization Review and Update Process

DCMA regularly reviews and updates the APM methodology and data sources, focusing on:

- Customer requirements and concerns;

- High-level guidance and policy;

- New information and sources that affect the model;

- New IT and other process improvements; and

- The evolving risk picture throughout the sector.

DCMA runs the APM in a secure computing environment to produce a final ranking of assets that constitutes the DIB CAL. Once the CAL is finalized and approved, and the APM results are verified, the ASD (HD&ASA) determines the scope of the annual assessment effort with associated remediation activities to follow.

Figure 4-1: Prioritization Factors, Sub Factors, and Weights

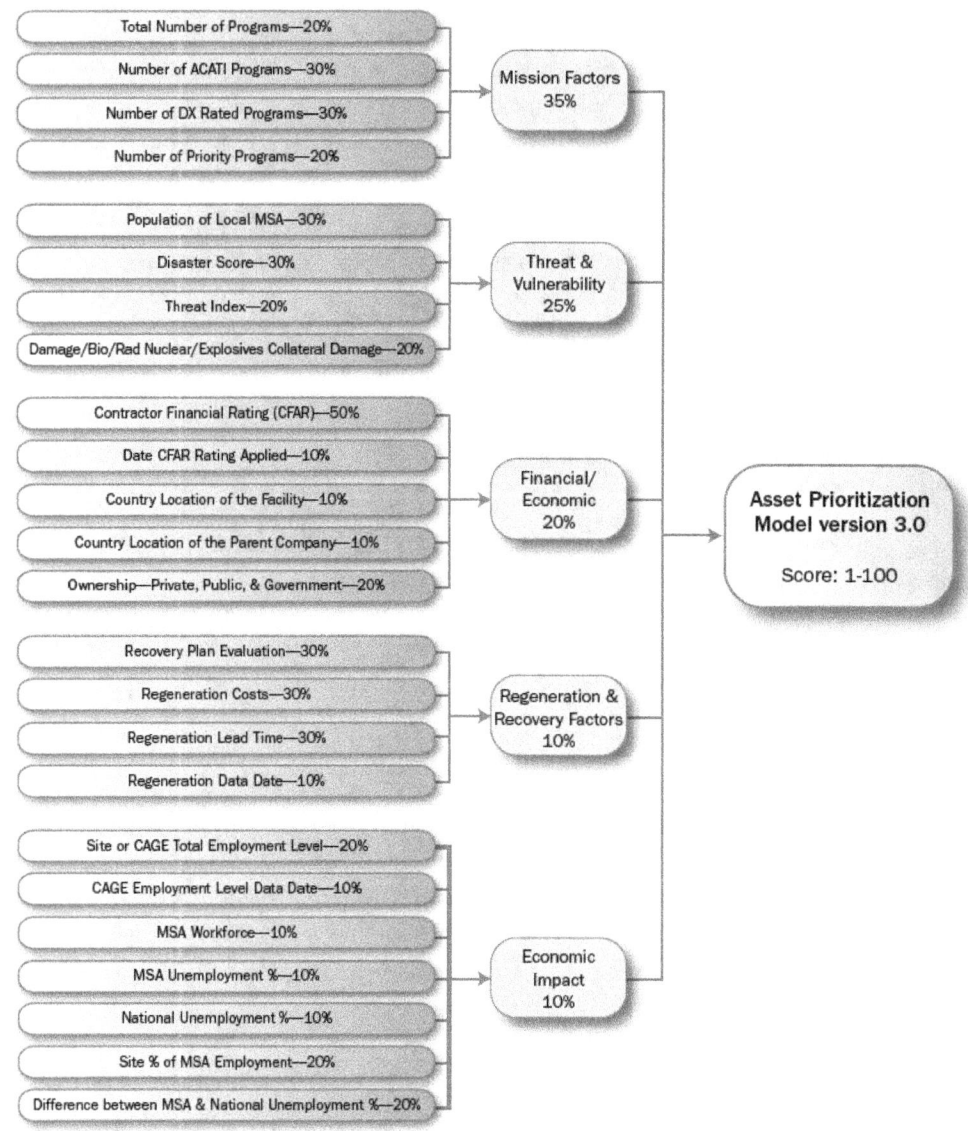

Each factor score = 100 by adding and weighting each sub factor. Then all factors are aggregated using the stated weights with a top score of 100.

5. Develop and Implement Protective Programs and Resilience Strategies

This chapter describes:

- How the DIB Sector develops and identifies the RMAs that derive from and support the program goals and objectives identified in chapter 1.

- How the DIB partnership develops, implements, and sustains voluntary best-practice protective programs and resilience strategies across the sector. Since publication of the 2007 SSP, the DIB has established sector-specific goals, objectives, implementation actions, and metrics. To support the shift to outcome-based metrics called for in the 2009 NIPP, DIB Sector partners determined that the principal focus should be on RMAs that prevent, deter, and mitigate threats to the sector. The DIB CIKR partners established RMAs discussed in this chapter, with outcome metrics collected and reported in the 2010 SAR. The sector has worked diligently and collaboratively to align risk programs with protection and resilience efforts, and will continue to adjust activities to sector needs.

5.1 Overview of Sector Protective Programs and Resilience Strategies

---

Cyber Highlights

The DoD DIB CS/IA program and its operational arm the DCISE under the DoD Cyber Crime Center facilitate a new level of threat information sharing to deter, respond to, assess the damage of, and recover from the ex-filtration or compromise of critical DoD information from unclassified DIB systems/networks.

The DSIE program involves DIB partners that share information on cyber attacks through use of a secure portal. Such sharing enables the DIB to identify and share attack attributes quickly so that DIB partners can immediately apply mitigation techniques to stop attacks. All information sharing is done in a multidirectional, networked, non-attributional method according to the NIPP and HSPD-7. This sharing now includes international sharing under a partnership with ADMIE in the United Kingdom. In addition, DSIE represents the DIB SCC in the cross-sector JCC pilot program.

5.1.1 DIB Sector Underlying Protection Approach

The composition of the DIB Sector continues to change with the increasing consolidation and globalization of the defense industry. This fact, along with the number of Federal, State, and local authorities having a situation-based role in CIKR protection and resilience, complicates the responsibility landscape. To clarify this situation, the following layered defense protection approach applies to DIB critical assets:

- **First level of protection:** DIB asset owners are responsible for the first level of protection. In addition to the inherent responsibility, to shareholders or creditors, many DoD contracts contain security requirements for contractors. Also, in the case of facilities that handle and store classified information, important regulatory and legal requirements are related to information protection.

- **Second level of protection:** As the seriousness of the threats escalates, local civilian law enforcement authorities augment and reinforce the efforts of asset owners in meeting CIKR-related protective responsibilities.

- **Third level of protection:** If the response from local authorities does not provide the necessary level of protection, State or Federal law enforcement authorities may be called upon to provide additional capability.

- **Fourth level of protection:** In more serious situations, a State governor may request other support under State Mutual Assistance Compacts, ask for Federal assistance, or employ the National Guard under his or her command and control to enhance protection and respond quickly to provide additional capability, with or without Federal funding. If ordered by the President or Secretary of Defense, with concurrence of the State Governor concerned, National Guard personnel could conduct this protective mission in a title 32 U.S. Code status.

- **Fifth level of protection:** When warranted, the President may direct employment of U.S. military forces to protect threatened DIB CIKR assets.

5.1.2 Goal Focused

The DIB partnership develops, implements, and sustains best-practice protective programs and resilience strategies based on extensive CIKR analysis, as well as the discussion and examination of validated partner concerns and issues drawn from years of experience and data. It is from this requirements foundation that the partnership developed shared sector goals and common RMAs to improve the protection and resilience of the DIB Sector. The sector partnership reviews its goals and risk mitigation activities annually at a minimum to determine whether adjustments are necessary.

Facilitated by the DIB SSA, the DIB partnership established five goals that underpin sector level protection programs and resilience strategies.

> **Sector Risk Management** identifies and assesses risk, and prioritizes DIB CIKR requiring risk mitigation.

> **Collaboration, Information Sharing, and Training** improves the understanding and the quality of information needed to mitigate risk effectively, as no one entity can accomplish this alone.

> **Personnel Security** addresses the trustworthiness and reliability of the DIB's people to perform their jobs with integrity.

> **Physical Security** addresses the need to manage the risk to property, the loss which would result in critical product and service disruption.

> **Information Security (CS/IA)** establishes a trust and process-based strategic framework to promote secure threat information sharing and improve the protection of unclassified DoD information residing or transiting non-DoD, DIB unclassified systems.

5.1.3 Partnership Dependent

Success in achieving DIB Sector goals and objectives depends on the combined efforts of the DIB partners. The partnership encompasses a broad set of relationships and coordinates structures necessary to develop, implement, and sustain protective programs and resilience strategies. The DIB SSA and SCC partners facilitate relationships with CIKR owners and operators through the governance structures established in the SSP.

The DIB SSA also collaborates in relationships with other government agencies, the private sector, laboratories, and academia to explore new concepts for protection and resilience, identify best-practice protection programs, coordinate Federal CIKR protection and resilience efforts, and determine DIB dependencies on other infrastructure sector services.

5.2 Cybersecurity/Information Assurance

DoD and members of the DIB Sector are implementing new collaborative mechanisms to support cybersecurity and information assurance, and plan to continue pursuing solutions in 2010–2011 to improve the protection of DoD information on unclassified DIB systems. One key element in DIB Sector cybersecurity planning and execution is DoD's DIB CS/IA program. The program, a premier example of public-private partnership, is facilitating a new level of cyber threat information sharing to deter, respond to, assess the damage of, and recover from the ex-filtration or compromise of sensitive DoD information on unclassified DIB systems.

The DoD DIB CS/IA program, launched as a pilot in 2007 is a collaborative effort between DoD and qualified CDCs. The program's mission is to protect critical, unclassified DoD program and technology information resident on, or transiting, DIB unclassified systems and networks. The DoD DIB CS/IA program office led by the ASD (NII)/DoD CIO oversees the program for DoD. The program is voluntary on the part of private sector members of the DIB and is executed at the corporate level under a bilateral agreement between the DoD CIO and individual DIB companies. The program's current success has led to its adoption by DHS as a model for cyber threat information sharing with other CIKR sectors.

The DCISE, an organizational construct under DoD Cyber Crime Center (DC3), was created to facilitate and support execution of DIB CS/IA activities. DCISE is the program's operational center for cyber threat information sharing and reporting, and is responsible for fusion, analysis, production, and dissemination of cyber threat products, as well as for receiving voluntary reports on cyber incidents on DIB unclassified systems/networks. DCISE implements an information-sharing framework for transmitting unclassified information through use of a public key infrastructure including DoD-approved External Certificate Authority certificates, and for transmitting classified information up to the SECRET level (DIBNet-S) through a secure system that is Defense Security Service certified and accredited.

The DoD DIB CS/IA program and DC3/DCISE support the development and execution of the DHS National Cyber Incident Response Plan (NCIRP) and participate in the development and execution of cybersecurity scenarios for CyberStorm III (CSIII) and other national-level exercises. DC3 will virtually participate in CSIII and the National Cybersecurity and Communications Integration Center (NCCIC).

The functional cybersecurity and information assurance expertise within the DoD DIB CS/IA program (ASD (NII)/DoD CIO) supports DIB Sector cybersecurity and execution of SSA responsibilities. Elements of the DIB CS/IA program directly support implementation of DIB SSP Goal 5, "Cyber Security, Assurance and Protection," and its associated RMAs and metrics. The DoD DIB CS/IA program participates in the DIB Sector GCC, GCC-SCC Information Sharing Working Group, and CSCSWG and its metrics sub working group.

DIB CS/IA program plans for 2010–2011 continue to focus on program expansion and increased capabilities. Goal 5, and its RMAs, outcome metrics, and action steps, represent key agreed GCC and SCC DIB Sector plans for 2010–2011. In addition, the DoD DIB CS/IA program plans for 2010–2011 include the following elements that directly or indirectly support Goal 5:

- 2010–2011 DIB CS/IA program.

- Continue to improve CS/IA measures to protect unclassified DoD program or technology information residing on or transiting DIB unclassified systems or networks. Accomplish this through cyber threat information sharing between DoD and DIB partners, IA measures, and identifying new technologies that enable detection, prevention, and response to cyber intrusions.

- Assess technological (and intellectual property) losses when unclassified Critical Program Information is lost, and support changes in contract language through FAR and DFAR modifications to mitigate further losses.

- Continue to leverage the results of specific cyber threat sharing and incident reporting to generate valuable real-time data that can be assessed and distributed (without company attribution) to participating DIB members.

- Continue phased transition of DIBNet to the DISA infrastructure.

- Continue risk assessment and mitigation activities through DCISE operations and DoD cyber intrusion damage assessment activities, and incorporate findings into alerts, cyber intrusion damage assessment reports, and other appropriate threat information products in support of improved cyber incident detection, prevention, and response actions.

- Continue to extend program to qualified CDCs in support of increased threat awareness, incident reporting, and protection of program and technology information.

- Partner with DHS in its adoption of the DoD DIB CS/IA program cyber threat information-sharing model.

- Expand and mature the DoD DIB CS/IA cyber threat information-sharing process.

- Continue to support development of acquisition and contracting policy to update the FAR and DFARS as appropriate, and to implement specific information protection language in defense contracts. Support the public meeting for the Advance Notice of Proposed Rulemaking and the public comment period.

- Support DIB Sector cybersecurity efforts enabling long-term protective planning for cyber elements and support DIB Sector efforts in characterizing DIB cyber elements and identifying cyber infrastructures, functions, or elements; identifying cyber dependencies and interdependencies; and prioritizing DIB cyber programs and initiatives, as appropriate. (ref DoDD 3020.40 and DoDI 5205.13)

- Measure progress of cybersecurity metrics.

- Continue to implement program in allowing eligible private sector employees to enroll at the Defense Cyber Investigations Training Academy at the Defense Cyber Crime Center in accordance with the National Defense Authorization Act for FY2010.

Defense Security Information Exchange – A partnership within the DIB

The DIB has developed DSIE, an industry-only cyber organization through the DIB SCC. DSIE has two levels of engagement. Its Strategic Subcommittee has engaged in an agreement with the ADMIE in the United Kingdom. Additionally, the DSIE represents the DIB SCC as a member in the JCC pilot program with the NSTAC and is a member of CSCSWG. The committee provides representation to the DIB from DHS and DOJ cyber programs through those sectors. The committee also shares techniques and tools to protect the DIB. The Tactical Subcommittee has engaged people at the DIB companies whose responsibility includes the protection of DIB networks and information systems. By using a mutual NDA and a secure portal, they share real-time attack and threat information among all DSIE members. Such sharing has enabled members to rapidly recognize cyber attacks and share cyber information rapidly, which in turn enables them to mitigate current attack campaigns from what DoD characterizes as the Advanced Persistent Threat (APT).

DSIE has participated in development of the pilot NSTAC JCC. The DSIE member companies who are also NSTAC companies are funding a 24/7 watch with the FS-ISAC to share cyber threat information. The ultimate goal is to have the JCC pilot become the industry representative of the NCCIC, in which DSIE would participate as the DIB SCC representative of the NCCIC.

- DSIE is now operational with a budget and staffing requirements to support the NCCIC.

- DSIE is also testing various event correlation products to provide a better product to DIB members for developing cyber information for sharing in cross-sector analyses.

- Expand and mature the DIB SCC DSIE cyber threat information-sharing process.

5.3 Determining the Need for Protective Programs and Resilience Strategies

The DIB Sector emphasizes prevention and protection against a broad spectrum of threats and hazards while recognizing the vagaries of most threats and the predictability of many natural hazards. The sector has various methods and tools developed under government and private sector auspices to support incident response. The DIB partners continue to explore ways to share information relevant to their roles from preparation through recovery.

Specific needs are subject to examination by DoD and DIB member companies. The following are among the options that one or more DIB partners may take to determine the need for a new protective program or a change to an existing program.

- DoD may collaborate with DIB CIKR asset owners to examine the cost/benefit associated with additional measures needed to protect critical service and product delivery consistent with DoD policy.

- DCIP awareness visits are an opportunity to include local law enforcement and State emergency first responders to strengthen relationships, security, and preparedness. By combining multiple perspectives, local threat and hazard information, and the specialized knowledge of DIB CIKR owners and operators, relationships will yield more robust remediation plans and implementation actions.

- DoD will collaborate with DIB CIKR owners and operators to reduce risk from an attack or hazard. DoD will share best practices and tools to make risk reduction easier for owners and operators.

- When appropriate, DoD will collaborate with owners/operators to determine jointly the steps necessary to reduce risk consistent with DoD policy. DoD and CIKR owners/operators will decide jointly which additional measures will be instituted, and develop a strategy to allocate the costs associated with this effort.

DoD and DIB asset owners and operators may consider using the Defense Priorities and Allocations System (DPAS) (15 CFR Part 700), expediting delivery of industrial resources supporting protection or restoration of a DIB asset to reduce potential interruptions to DIB operations, including in emergency conditions. DoD implements its DPAS rating authority as a standard clause in most of its contracts and orders for industrial resources. In instances where multiple DIB CIKR are threatened/damaged, DPAS support would likely be in accordance with the DIB Sector Assurance Plan. This plan outlines an approach that focuses on steps to identify a list of critical assets that, if damaged or destroyed, will result in unacceptable consequences. The DPAS may also be used to support military or critical infrastructure assistance to any foreign nation.

5.4 Protective Program/Resilience Strategy Implementation

Central elements of the DCIP continue to be risk assessments and risk reduction efforts, along with outreach to the private sector. These primary activities have matured and include the following major umbrella activities: (1) perform sector characterization; (2) identify and prioritize critical assets; and (3) perform assessments. The DIB will continue its work with CIKR owners/operators and other sectors to determine dependencies and interdependencies among sectors. Ongoing efforts will continue to enhance geospatial information sharing and a better understanding of linkages and dependencies with DCIP stakeholders. The DIB SSA continues to address risks associated with dependence on IT and cyber systems essential to DoD mission success.

5.4.1 Voluntary Protective Program/Resilience Options

Implementing DIB protection programs and resilience strategies consists of the following elements:

- Developing plans that address remediation of vulnerabilities, mitigation, and interdependencies, and consequence management;

- Developing protective capabilities, commitments, and forces internal and external to a facility;

- Using information garnered from the analysis and assessment processes;

- Providing continuous monitoring of changes in threats, operating environment, criticality, and factors effecting consequence management; executing agreed remediation and mitigation strategies; and determining the degree of progress and impact of local, State, and Federal risk mitigation measures at the facility;

- Contingency planning and execution;

- Referral and reporting;

- Education, awareness, and training; and

- Processes, tools, and resources to improve DIB Sector protection and resilience.

The DIB CIKR owner is responsible for providing asset security and preparedness. The CIKR owner usually accomplishes this through normal business processes, such as business continuity planning and programs. For cleared facilities, the DIB SSA-led criticality notification process conveys the criticality determination, solicits and confirms company and facility agreement to engage in the process, and provides recommendations on immediate and longer term actions. The Office of the ASD (OASD) (HD&ASA), working with other appropriate DoD offices, oversees the notification process. DoD ensures that information about criticality determination is shared with the companies responsible for protecting the CIKR.

If DoD identifies an unacceptable level of risk associated with the critical DIB asset, DoD leadership may explore one or more of the following actions in collaboration with the DIB CIKR owner:

- Conduct remediation activities to minimize exposure or eliminate exploitable vulnerabilities;

- Develop mitigation options to execute contingency plans or temporarily strengthen security measures;

- Develop response plans to manage scenario-specific emergencies;

- Prepare for an infrastructure-related incident (exercise contingency plans) and integrate these plans into other sector exercise and evaluation programs; and/or

- Develop reconstitution tradeoff analyses (e.g., outline alternative sources of supply).

DoD or the DIB CIKR owner may partially or fully employ the following practices to enhance CIKR protection and resilience:

- Coordinate with public and private sector organizations to enhance the security of supporting DIB assets. Critical DIB asset owners and those who contract for non-DoD infrastructure services and products will monitor risk. As potential threats and operating conditions change, DIB partners may review previous risk analyses to determine whether remediation or mitigation recommendations require update.

- Request local and State law enforcement, and other local and State emergency resources, in addition to its own resources to meet emergency needs. State and local law enforcement and other emergency responders will monitor factors within their jurisdictions. They provide advice, assistance, warning, and alert; incorporate the facility into emergency planning; and prioritize assistance for incident response and other services.

- DoD policies and procedures ensure prompt and appropriate sharing of critical asset and facility information with FBI headquarters, which may provide information to its field offices for incorporation in planning and operations. The FBI will share threat information regarding the facility consistent with all laws, regulations, and other applicable legal authorities, and other FBI polices in support of DoD industrial security and counterintelligence officials, and brief DoD officials and other key partners when requested.

- The FBI and DoD may also use the Joint Terrorism Task Force structure for information sharing pursuant to all legal requirements, authorities, and other FBI policies to help protect the critical DIB asset, subject to restrictions that DoD may place on dissemination of the asset information.

The Federal Emergency Management Agency (FEMA) may be able to provide emergency assistance in certain situations, upon request of the DIB CIKR owner/operator and in coordination with State and local government officials. DoD will collaborate with owners and operators to evaluate that assistance and other services those organizations may offer to enable better informed decisions regarding:

1. How the facility should interface with government officials;

2. What information the DIB CIKR owner/operator should provide to the government;

3. What assistance the owner/operator should seek related to its status as a DIB CIKR; and

4. How DoD should proceed to promote and facilitate such assistance across the DIB CIKR owner/operator community.

Other SSAs, DHS, and the national intelligence community may have information directly relevant to DIB CIKR. DoD is collaborating with its partners to ensure full integration and appropriate sharing of information that may adversely affect DIB CIKR protection or resilience.

DoD components will execute their assigned roles as prescribed in DoD policy. DoD will promptly share information regarding the potential endangerment of DIB CIKR with partners that have protection roles identified in this plan.

Combatant Commands plan and coordinate military force deployment and protection of designated DoD critical facilities within their respective areas of responsibility. DoD will develop procedures for contingency military protection of DIB CIKR, and identify the responsibilities of the military departments, Combatant Commanders, and National Guard forces under Title 10 or Title 32 of United States Code. Combatant Commanders will coordinate with the appropriate U.S. ambassadors regarding all protection plans and activities associated with DIB CIKR outside the United States.

5.4.2 DIB Sector RMAs

Efforts continue to better align DCIP processes with DIB SSA and DIB Sector responsibilities under the NIPP. Culminating in 2008, the DIB Sector partners issued a hierarchical set of goals, objectives, implementation actions, and metrics. Chapter 1 highlights the goals and their associated objectives. Subsequent to this issuance, the NIPP revision of 2009 established uniform guidance for the use of RMAs. The DIB partners were able to categorize various implementation actions into RMA categories (table 5.1).

The DIB Sector has identified 16 RMAs that will focus on protection and resilience. An RMA is an activity conducted by a DIB CIKR partner; the DIB SSA, GCC, SCC, or member association; a DIB CIKR owner/operator; or a combination that contributes to sector protection and resilience. These activities become metrics to evaluate progress against DIB Sector goals and objectives.

5.5 Monitoring Program Implementation

The metrics aligned to each implementation action will be used to monitor progress in the various RMA efforts. Chapter 6 describes this monitoring activity in more detail.

Table 5-1: Key RMAs Associated with Five DIB CIKR Goals and Related Implementation Actions—for Planned 2010 Implementation

RMA1: Business Continuity Plans – CIKR owners/operators establish and employ business continuity plans for their own assets and in conjunction with critical suppliers.	Goal Addressed: 1
Implementation Actions	**Who Is Responsible**
1C1: DIB CIKR owners and operators develop and maintain comprehensive and effective emergency, disaster, and business continuity plans.	SCC
1C3: DIB CIKR owners and operators develop business/operations continuity plans in conjunction with their respective suppliers.	SCC

RMA 2: CIKR Asset Identification and Prioritization – SSA develops, coordinates, and approves annual listing of DIB CIKR and notifies asset owners and operators of changes in criticality.	Goal Addressed: 1
Implementation Actions	**Who Is Responsible**
1A1: SSA develops, coordinates, and approves DIB CIKR listing.	SSA
1A2: SSA notifies affected DIB CIKR owners and operators of changes in criticality.	SSA

RMA 3: DCIP Resilience Guide and Best Practices – SSA maintains and distributes DCIP Resilience Guide, and owners and operators develop, share, and make use of a set of "best practices."	Goals Addressed: 2, 4
Implementation Actions	**Who Is Responsible**
2C1: SSA develops, issues, and maintains a comprehensive Defense Critical Infrastructure Resilience Guide that includes DIB Sector requirements.	SSA
2C2: DIB SCC, in collaboration with GCC, establishes a best practices guide to identify, review, and share risk mitigation measures throughout the areas of physical, human, and cyber threats and vulnerabilities.	SSA/SCC
4B4: SSA, working with DIB SCC, catalogs and publishes risk reduction measures, best practices, and vulnerabilities.	SSA/SCC

RMA 4: Dependency Analysis – CIKR partners work together to conduct dependency analysis and identify local dependencies.	Goal Addressed: 1
Implementation Actions	**Who Is Responsible**
1D1: DIB CIKR owners and operators identify dependencies through the risk assessment process.	SCC
1D2: DIB Sector partners collaborate to develop dependency analysis and identification methodologies.	SCC

RMA 5: DIB Asset Local Information Sharing – SSA works with owners and operators to develop local networks that facilitate tactical threat information sharing.	Goals Addressed: 1, 4
Implementation Actions	**Who Is Responsible**
1D3: DIB CIKR owners and operators share dependency information and mitigation measures with SSA and other sector partners in an appropriate, commercially sensitive manner.	SSA/SCC
1E2: SSA identifies appropriate military/defense points of contact in law enforcement and counterintelligence organizations to support establishment of local threat information-sharing networks.	SSA
4B3: SSA, working with other government partners, implements awareness program that familiarizes DIB CIKR owners and operators with Federal, State, and local first responder structures, processes, and resources relevant to aiding risk reduction efforts.	SSA

RMA 6: DIB Cybersecurity, Assurance, and Protection – SSA identifies standards and guidelines for protecting DIB electronic information and communication systems, networks, and control systems; defines the sensitivity level and impact of loss or compromise of information involving DIB CIKR; and publishes information assurance guidance. DIB CIKR owners and operators adopt industry standards and regulations, implement training, assess risk to CIKR information, and develop plans to mitigate the risks. DIB Sector partners develop and implement methodologies for information sharing in a dynamic information sharing network designed to provide timely, actionable threat information, assessments, and warnings to public and private sector partners.	Goal Addressed: 5
Implementation Actions	**Who Is Responsible**
5A1: SSA provides policy and guidance on the sensitivity and resulting impact of loss, corruption, or unauthorized access of the information involving DIB CIKR, and publishes an information assurance guidance.	SSA
5A2: DIB CIKR owners and operators conduct self-assessments of the risk to CIKR information related to critical DIB assets identified by the SSA.	SCC
5A3: DIB CIKR owners and operators implement awareness training for employees responsible for information protection.	SCC

5A4: DIB owners and operators identify and adopt commonly accepted industry standards and government regulations for the protection of information.	SCC
5A5: DIB owners and operators develop a plan to mitigate risks associated with this information.	SCC
5B1: SSA identifies standards and guidelines for the protection of DIB information and communication systems, networks, and control systems.	SSA
5B2: DIB owners and operators apply IA standards and guidelines to mitigate risks to these systems, networks, and control systems commensurate with the level of protection needed for the information at risk.	SCC
5B3: DIB owners and operators implement awareness training for employees responsible for protection of the systems.	SCC
5B4: DIB Sector partners develop and implement methodologies for information sharing in a comprehensive, multitiered, dynamic, information-sharing network designed to provide timely and actionable threat information, assessments, and warnings to public and private sector partners.	SSA

RMA 7: DIB Sector Outreach Activities – SSA works with sector partners to establish a training and education strategy, conduct conferences and seminars, and conduct individual CIKR asset awareness visits.	Goal Addressed: 2
Implementation Actions	**Who Is Responsible**
2B1: SSA leads the DIB GCC and SCC in developing and issuing a comprehensive DIB CIKR training and education strategy.	SSA/SCC
2B2: SSA leads the DIB GCC and SCC in sponsoring defense-critical infrastructure training conferences, seminars, symposiums, and workshops for CIKR owners and operators.	SSA
2B3: SSA conducts onsite DCIP awareness training at DIB CIKR sites.	SSA

RMA 8: Exercise Programs – CIKR owners/operators and SSA participate in exercises to enhance emergency preparedness and reliability of critical capability.	Goal Addressed: 1
Implementation Actions	**Who Is Responsible**
1C2: DIB CIKR owners and operators and SSA participate in exercises to enhance emergency preparedness and reliability of critical capability.	SSA/SCC

RMA 9: Incident Reporting and Response Information Sharing – SSA works with DHS to provide DIB asset owners and operators with a simple, rapid incident communication process that facilitates reporting and response resource information flow.	Goal Addressed: 1
Implementation Actions	**Who Is Responsible**
1E3: SSA works with DHS to provide DIB asset owners and operators with a simple, rapid incident communication process that facilitates reporting and response resource information flow.	SSA

RMA 10: Information Sharing Requirements Generation – DIB CIKR partners collaboratively develop information-sharing requirements.	Goal Addressed: 2
Implementation Actions	**Who Is Responsible**
2A1: DIB Sector CIKR partners collaboratively develop information-sharing requirements.	SSA/SCC

RMA 11: Insider Threat Guidance and Application – SCC and owners and operators develop and implement security awareness training, including insider threat awareness, and deploy systems/methods for periodic rescreening, identifying, and reporting anomalous behavior.	Goal Addressed: 3
Implementation Actions	**Who Is Responsible**
3B1: DIB SCC develops a baseline guide for insider threat education and awareness training.	SCC
3B2: DIB CIKR owners and operators provide new hire orientation, periodic training, and ongoing awareness regarding insider threats.	SCC
3B3: DIB CIKR owners and operators establish a methodology and channel for employee reporting of suspected insider threats.	SCC
3B4: DIB CIKR owners and operators develop and implement program for periodic personnel screening and identifying anomalous behavior.	SCC

RMA 12: Local Security Awareness Training – SCC leads development of an outline with references and standards for awareness training throughout the sector and owners and operators implement training at the asset level.	Goal Addressed: 2
Implementation Actions	**Who Is Responsible**
2B4: DIB SCC develops an outline with references and standards for awareness training throughout the sector.	SCC
2B5: DIB CIKR owners and operators develop and implement local security awareness training for employees at DIB critical asset sites.	SCC

RMA 13: Mission Assurance Assessments and Follow-up – SSA, in cooperation with CIKR partners, schedules and carries out Mission Assurance Assessments; owners and operators participate in follow-up and implementation reporting after one year.	Goals Addressed: 1, 4
Implementation Actions	**Who Is Responsible**
1B2: SSA coordinates assessment plans with DIB owners and operators, and budgets and accomplishes Mission Assurance Assessments annually.	SSA
4B2: DIB CIKR owners and operators participate in one-year follow-up reviews of Mission Assurance Assessments annually.	SCC

RMA 14: Personnel Screening Guidance and Application – SSA, in collaboration with DIB partners, publishes personnel screening and access control guidance document; owners and operators apply the guidance at CIKR facilities.	Goal Addressed: 3
Implementation Actions	**Who Is Responsible**
3A1: SSA, in collaboration with DIB Sector partners, publishes personnel screening and access control guidance.	SSA/SCC
3A2: DIB CIKR owners and operators, at a minimum, apply personnel screening and access control guidance.	SSA/SCC

RMA 15: Risk Response Planning and Implementation – CIKR owners and operators carry out risk response and mitigation planning based on assessments, and budget such activities appropriately.	Goals Addressed: 1, 4
Implementation Actions	**Who Is Responsible**
1C4: DIB CIKR owners and operators plan and implement mitigation actions to eliminate vulnerabilities and reduce unacceptable levels of risk they can influence.	SCC
1C5: SSA plans and implements mitigation actions to eliminate vulnerabilities and unacceptable levels of risk for those vulnerabilities associated with numerous programs and sectors for which no one DIB CIKR owner/operator can influence risk reduction.	SSA
4B1: DIB CIKR owners and operators develop response options for known threats and vulnerabilities.	SCC
4C1: DIB CIKR owners and operators incorporate risk response action resource requirements into their annual budget development process.	SCC
4C2: DIB CIKR owners and operators apply lessons learned from participation in exercises to reduce risk of physical damage/destruction to their facilities.	SCC

RMA 16: Self-Assessment Tool – SSA leads other CIKR partners in developing a risk self-assessment tool.	Goals Addressed: 1, 4
Implementation Actions	**Who Is Responsible**
1B1: SSA, in collaboration with CIKR owners and operators, develops and implements a risk self-assessment tool.	SSA/SCC
4A1: SSA leads GCC and SCC in establishing a common assessment methodology based on industry best practices, standards, and regulatory/statutory requirements.	SSA
4A2: DIB CIKR owners and operators plan, budget, and accomplish self-assessments for DIB critical assets as part of their business continuity planning operations.	SCC

6. Measure Effectiveness

This chapter describes how the DIB partnership measures the effectiveness of its RMAs and the processes to support continuous improvement of CIKR protection and resilience. The DIB Sector has collected feedback on metrics that helps evaluate progress against the broader sector goals. For example, DoD conducts the voluntary CIP-MAA and awareness visits that provide an opportunity to assess and collect information from CIKR owners and operators. Data collected through these programs will be aggregated to identify gaps and trends to better address protection and resilience measures. The DIB partnership will work to improve mitigation efforts by prioritizing risk strategies that consistently reflect CIKR priorities and remain flexible to respond to changing circumstances.

Performance and outcome metrics enable DoD and the DIB to establish accountability, document actual performance, facilitate the diagnosis of problems, promote effective management, make decisions, and provide feedback to senior decisionmakers in the DIB partnership. The metrics are aligned with DIB Sector goals and objectives and have evolved from descriptive and output data to outcome metrics. The 2010 DIB SAR includes the first reporting of DIB metrics. The DIB GCC and SCC conducted independent reviews, and together reported progress made against specific RMAs. This enables the sector to measure its effectiveness and plan improvements.

Cyber Highlights

Cybersecurity is a part of DIB Sector goals, objectives, implementation actions, and supporting metrics; findings will guide future cyber activities.

The process of developing DIB metrics began with subject matter experts from the private sector, trade associations, and government agencies that collaborated to develop a consensus set of defined metrics that correspond to sector goals, objectives, and implementation actions. These metrics will continue to evolve as the DIB GCC-SCC partnership matures and a common perspective of plans and expectations emerges. The GCC and SCC will review, monitor, update, and approve metrics during annual reviews of the metrics program.

Cybersecurity is included in the metrics development, analysis, and reporting process. Associated cyber outcome metrics are represented in the sector's Goal 5 and RMA 6 consistent with an October 2007 Government Accountability Office (GAO) report[2] and current DHS SSP guidance. The metrics primarily support Goal 5, as itemized in table 6-1. Cyber metrics measure the beneficial effects of cybersecurity implementation actions.

---

[2] In 2007, GAO analyzed each NIPP SSP and, in October, released a report that evaluated coverage of cyber concerns in the 2007 SSPs. DHS, in its process for the triennial rewrite and reissue of the SSPs, provided guidance that the 2010 SSPs should detail the cyber elements of sector infrastructure and describe ongoing efforts to enhance and maintain cybersecurity in the sector.

The cyber metrics planned for 2010–2011 represent a convergence of actions from across the sector. Some actions will take place sector-wide directly under the broad NIPP CIKR construct (e.g., SSA, GCC, and SCC). Other actions are under a specific framework, wherein DoD and eligible CDCs that have signed bilateral agreements with DoD are sharing threat information through trust and process-based partnerships. In each case, metrics are being established to determine benefits (or gaps) and help identify and prioritize cybersecurity risk mitigation.

DIB Sector partners will continue progress toward refining and collecting information against the metrics, and instituting a simplified approach to capture reporting information. The process consolidates metrics into two main categories:

- **National Coordinator Progress Indicators**. These describe DHS/IP efforts to support NIPP and SSP related activities.
- **Sector Progress Indicators**. These measure the progress made by the sector, as well as the effectiveness of RMAs within the sector.

The 2010 DIB SSP implements comprehensive, GCC and SCC coordinated and integrated goals, objectives, implementation actions, RMAs and metrics, which identify the roadmap to achieve maximum success.

6.1 Process for Measuring Effectiveness

The DIB GCC and SCC are responsible for jointly developing, validating, and updating DIB Sector metrics. DoD records and reports DIB Sector metrics annually to DHS through the SAR.

A primary indicator used to measure CIKR protection progress is the number of successfully completed CIP-MAAs and awareness visits. During FY 2009, there were 30 awareness visits conducted and 20 on-site assessments were completed. The cumulative totals through FY2009 are 144 and 52, respectively. The current proposed schedule will include approximately 25–30 CIP-MAAs annually, with continued emphasis on dependency analysis, to meet its goal by 2013.

DoD will improve CIP-MAA capabilities through development of an automated assessment tool to increase efficiency and enable extraction of relevant data for trending purposes for both industry and DoD. The DIB SSA will work in conjunction with DIB CIKR owners and operators to develop local networks that facilitate tactical threat information sharing. The DIB GCC and SCC will work closely this year, as stated in RMA10 to identify information-sharing requirements in an all-hazards environment, including cyber-related hazards. The DIB partnership will address several other implementation activities, such as:

- DIB SSA and SCC will participate in preplanning for the National Level Exercises for 2010 and 2011, with DIB owner and operator participation;
- DIB CIP 2010 Conference; and
- DIB SSA and SCC will implement awareness programs in 2010 and 2011 that familiarize CIKR owners and operators with Federal, State, and local first responder structures, processes, and resources relevant to aiding site risk reduction efforts.

In support of metrics reporting for the 2010 SAR, DoD and the DIB GCC and SCC will develop an approach to deploy specific DIB Sector metrics and gather data. This approach will identify how information is to be provided to the DIB regarding goals, objectives, and metrics; how data is reported, gathered, and assessed; and who tracks metrics and timelines for deploying and completing the metrics. The sector will conduct bi-annual reviews of outcome metrics at CIPAC meetings and determine the extent to which CIKR partners are achieving the sector outcomes for protection of critical DIB assets.

6.1.1 Process for Measuring Sector Progress

DIB Sector CIKR partners developed a set of metrics that pertain directly to implementation of the sector's protection and resilience goals. The metrics appear in the 2010 SAR. During the next year, CIKR owners and operators, through the SCC, will track 43 outcome-based metrics to measure progress in implementing protective programs and resilience strategies. In addition, in response to growing cybersecurity threats and reported incidents within the DIB CIKR community, the SSA, including the support of DoD DIB CS/IA program, and the SCC are implementing RMA 6 and applying metrics to measure the effectiveness of RMA 6. The DIB SSA continues to coordinate ongoing initiatives and leverages government threat detection and assessment capabilities to share timely information with CIKR owners and operators in a trusted environment.

6.1.2 Information Collection and Verification

The DIB GCC, in collaboration with the DIB SCC, continues to assess and verify progress data for core and DIB Sector metrics. The DIB GCC and SCC compile and analyze data gathered in support of specific metrics, as identified in the RMA table in chapter 5.

The DIB SCC will approve all DIB Sector data calls prior to issuance. The DIB SSA will request at least one data call annually to support preparation of the SAR to DHS until a controlled-access, Web-enabled server is deployed to support reporting needs. When the Web-enabled capability is operational, DIB asset owners/operators and other CIKR partners will post and query data as needed. The DIB GCC and SCC will jointly determine access authorities required to protect sensitive data.

To support the NIPP requirement to report metrics-based progress in the SAR, the GCC and SCC will annually assess the effectiveness of metrics, as well as progress against the goals, objectives, and implementation actions they measure. Both will assess owner/operator data submissions and monitor postings of owner/operator-provided metrics data on the DoD Web collection site. The DIB SSA will monitor contract performance with provisions that contribute to sector-specific goals and objectives.

6.1.3 Reporting

The DIB Sector will participate in the national annual reporting process led by DHS addressing:

- The SAR that provides an overall progress report for the sector as mapped against the national CIP goals for the DIB; and

- Best practices learned from implementation of successful DIB Sector programs and initiatives.

6.2 Using Metrics for Continuous Improvement

DIB Sector CIKR protection/resilience goals and associated performance metrics will continue to be refined and serve as the roadmap to further progress. The results of the metrics program will yield a definitive health assessment of the DIB Sector using a scorecard approach. These scorecard performance assessments, collaboratively implemented by the GCC and SCC, require the annual gathering of metrics information from DIB Sector stakeholders and subsequent analyses. The first annual scorecard review was accomplished in 2010, with the results reported to DHS in the DIB SAR. This information will be used to determine the effectiveness of actions already taken by the sector to improve sector resilience and will lead to identification of additional actions required to reduce risk. The 2010 performance assessment will serve as the baseline for measuring how effectively the sector is operating in the future.

DIB Sector Performance Measurement System

Scorecards are developed for each RMA, implementation action, objective, and goal to review and evaluate sector performance. Metrics describe DIB Sector partners progress and are used to revise plans.

- >75% completion = Green
- 75% - 25% completion = Yellow
- <25% completion = Red
- Not yet started = Black

Annual Reviews: Information is collected from in-depth self-evaluation scorecards and progress statements are developed by DIB Sector partners and reviewed/evaluated by the GCC and SCC during March–April annually. Self evaluations determine current status, corrective action, and the need to revise plans. Summary level evaluations are performed by GCC and SCC for each goal. Summary RMA evaluation results are reported to DHS.

Summary Level Evaluation Requirements:
- Descriptive Response
- Progress Status

Table 6-1: Implementation Actions and Outcome Metrics

Implementation Actions	Outcome Metrics
1A1: SSA develops, coordinates, and approves DIB CIKR listing.	1A1A: SSA solicits nominations for the CAL from the military departments, defense agencies, and DIB every fiscal year. 1A1B: SSA reviews, updates, and coordinates the CAL with SCC as part of the SAR process. 1A1C: SSA encourages the DIB to nominate assets, systems, networks, and facilities for designation as DIB CIKR. 1A1D: SSA implements automated asset identification mechanism.
1A2: SSA notifies affected DIB CIKR owners/operators of changes in criticality.	1A2A: SSA issues notification letters to DIB CIKR owners/operators within 30 days of approval of CAL annual update. 1A2B: SSA requests that un-cleared DIB CIKR owners/operators added to the CAL apply for clearance within 30 days of the CAL approval.
1B1: SSA, in collaboration with CIKR owners/operators, develops and implements a risk self-assessment tool.	1B1A: SSA and SCC agree on a minimum set of risk assessment tool requirements. 1B1B: GCC and SCC agree to hold a specific developer/acquirer accountable for producing an acceptable risk assessment tool.
1B2: SSA coordinates Mission Assurance Assessment plans with DIB owners/operators, and budgets and accomplishes the assessments annually.	1B2A: The SSA coordinates Mission Assurance Assessment plans with DIB owners and operators. 1B2B: Assessments meet or exceed the number planned.
1C1: DIB CIKR owners and operators develop and maintain comprehensive and effective emergency, disaster, and business continuity plans.	1C1A: DIB CIKR owners and operators acknowledge that they conform to accredited standards (e.g., ISO/PAS 22399) for plan development.
1C2: DIB CIKR owners and operators and SSA participate in exercises to enhance emergency preparedness and reliability of critical capability.	1C2A: DIB CIKR sites exercise plans annually and implement lessons learned and other identified improvement actions. Real emergency events, successfully mitigated, also satisfy the requirement.
1C3: DIB CIKR owners/operators develop business/operations continuity plans in conjunction with their suppliers.	1C3A: DIB CIKR sites report the development and exercising of business/operations continuity plans with their principal suppliers.
1C4: DIB CIKR owners and operators plan and implement mitigation actions to eliminate vulnerabilities and reduce unacceptable levels of risk.	1C4A: DIB CIKR sites report mitigation options (e.g., identify alternate sources of critical supplies or stockpile redundant capability where alternative sources do not exist). 1C4B: DIB CIKR owners and operators report the number and characteristics of risk mitigation actions they have taken.

1C5: SSA plans and implements mitigation actions to eliminate vulnerabilities and unacceptable levels of risk for those vulnerabilities associated with numerous programs and sectors for which no one DIB CIKR owner/operator can influence risk reduction.	1C5A: SSA identifies interdependencies for critical programs. 1C5B: SSA identifies unacceptable levels of risk related to interdependencies identified. 1C5C: SSA reports number of plans to mitigate unacceptable risk.
1D1: DIB CIKR owners and operators identify dependencies through the risk assessment process.	1D1A: Number of DIB partners reporting dependencies through their risk assessment processes. The outcome metric is the percentage reporting.
1D2: DIB Sector partners collaborate to develop dependency analysis and identification methodologies.	1D2A: DIB SCC forms a committee to engage DIB partners in developing dependency identification methodologies and strategic business resilience strategies. 1D2B: DIB partners assist SSA in identifying key critical dependencies that might require further analysis. The outcome metric is the percentage participating.
1D3: DIB CIKR owners and operators share dependency information and mitigation measures with SSA and other sector partners in an appropriate, commercially sensitive manner.	1D3A: SSA engages the PCII Program Office to categorically include key DIB infrastructure dependencies and mitigation measures as PCII. 1D3B: The DIB SCC and GCC information-sharing subcommittees develop an information-sharing process consistent with the protections mandated by the PCII Program Office.
1E2: SSA identifies appropriate military/defense points of contact in law enforcement and counterintelligence organizations to support establishment of local threat information-sharing networks.	1E2A: SSA develops contact list.
1E3: SSA works with DHS to provide DIB asset owners and operators with a simple, rapid incident communication process that facilitates incident reporting and response resource information flow.	1E3A: DoD/DHS/DIB CIKR capability provided to promote an effective two-way information-sharing capability. 1E3B: Barriers identified to SSA threat sharing are resolved to enable information sharing with DIB CIKR owners and operators in support of DIB incident reporting and response.
2A1: DIB Sector partners collaboratively develop information-sharing requirements.	2A1A: GCC and SCC establish standing committees to develop information-sharing requirements, handling, and exchange procedures under the CIPAC umbrella. 2A1B: GCC and SCC approve an information-sharing requirements document.
2B1: SSA leads DIB GCC and SCC in developing and issuing a comprehensive CIKR training and education strategy.	2B1A: SSA and SCC develop a consensus-based set of education and training requirements for security awareness. 2B1B: SSA develops security awareness training and education that is responsive to consensus-based requirements.
2B2: SSA leads DIB GCC and SCC in sponsoring defense-critical infrastructure training conferences, seminars, symposia, and workshops for CIKR owners and operators.	2B2A: SSA sponsors annual training and related conferences.

2B3: SSA conducts onsite DCIP awareness training at DIB CIKR sites.	2B3A: SSA conducts annual security awareness training at critical DIB sites.
2B4: DIB SCC develops an outline with references and standards for awareness training throughout the sector.	2B4A: DIB SCC issues updates to references and standards.
2B5: DIB CIKR owners and operators develop and implement local security awareness training for employees at critical assets.	2B5A: DIB sites conduct local security awareness training annually.
2C1: SSA develops, issues, and maintains the comprehensive Defense Critical Infrastructure Resilience Guide that includes DIB Sector requirements.	2C1A: SSA publishes the Defense Critical Infrastructure Resilience Guide.
2C2: DIB SCC, collaborating with GCC, establishes a best practices guide to identify, review, and share risk mitigation measures for physical, human, and cyber threats and vulnerabilities.	2C1B: SSA incorporates information collected from assessments performed by the DIB Sector into updates of the Defense Critical Infrastructure Resilience Guide.
	2C2A: SCC publishes a best practices guide annually, incorporating sanitized CIP-MAA results and owner/operator self-assessments.
3A1: SSA, in collaboration with DIB Sector partners, publishes a personnel screening and access control guidance document.	3A1A: GCC and SCC publish a vetted personnel screening process guide for distribution to critical DIB assets.
3A2: DIB CIKR owners and operators, at a minimum, apply personnel screening and access control guidance.	3A2A: Self-assessment and CIP-MAA processes evaluate the DIB owners and operators' personnel screening guidance for conformance to minimal acceptable standards/best practices.
	3A2B: DIB owners/operators report they are applying personnel screening and access control guidelines.
3B1: DIB SCC develops a baseline guide for insider threat education and awareness training.	3B1A: SCC has vetted and distributed the Infrastructure Insider Threat Awareness Guide.
3B2: DIB CIKR owners and operators provide new hire orientation, periodic training, and ongoing awareness regarding insider threats.	3B2A: DIB owners/operators report they are providing new hire orientation.
	3B2B: DIB owners/operators report they are providing periodic training and ongoing awareness regarding insider threats.
3B3: DIB CIKR owners and operators establish a methodology and channel for employee reporting of suspected insider threats.	3B3A: Self-assessment and CIP-MAA processes evaluate the DIB owners and operators' employee reporting processes for insider threats for conformance to minimal acceptable standards/best practices.
	3b3B: DIB owners and operators report they have established processes for employee reporting of suspected insider threats.

3B4: DIB CIKR owners and operators develop and implement program for periodic personnel screening and identifying anomalous behavior.	3B4A: Self-assessment and CIP-MAA processes evaluate the DIB owners and operators' employee compliance/behavior monitoring processes for conformance to minimal acceptable standards/best practices. 3B4B: DIB owners and operators report they have implemented a program for periodic personnel screening and identifying anomalous behavior.
4A1: SSA lead GCC and SCC in establishing a common assessment methodology based on industry best practices, standards, and regulatory/statutory requirements.	4A1A: SSA publishes a common assessment methodology.
4A2: DIB CIKR owners and operators plan, budget, and accomplish self-assessments for DIB critical assets as part of their business continuity planning operations.	4A2A: DIB owners and operators report completion of self-assessments.
4B1: DIB CIKR owners and operators develop response options for known threats and vulnerabilities.	4B1A: DIB owners and operators report they have developed response options based on results of self-assessments or external assessment. The outcome metric is the percentage of the total.
4B2: DIB CIKR owners and operators participate in one-year follow-up reviews of Mission Assurance Assessments annually.	4B2A: Externally assessed DIB CIKR sites report risk response options implemented.
4B3: SSA, working with other government partners, implements awareness program that familiarizes DIB CIKR owners and operators with Federal, State, and local first responder structures, processes, and resources relevant to aiding site reduction efforts.	4B3A: DIB CIKR sites report familiarization with structures, processes, and resources aiding risk reduction. The response is expressed as a percentage.
4B4: SSA, working with DIB SCC, catalogs and publishes risk reduction measures, best practices, and vulnerabilities.	4B4A: Best practices compendium published.
4C1: DIB CIKR owners and operators incorporate risk response action resource requirements into their annual budget development processes.	4C1A: Owners and operators report risk response action resource requirements are properly budgeted.
4C2: DIB CIKR owners and operators apply lessons learned from participation in exercises to reduce risk of physical damage/destruction to their facility.	4C2A: Owners and operators report that lessons learned have been properly applied from exercises into overall plans to reduce risk.
5A1: SSA provides policy and guidance on the sensitivity level and resulting impact of loss, corruption, or unauthorized access of information involving DIB CIKR, and publishes information assurance guidance.	5A1A: SSA achieves National Archives and Records Administration and DoD—established milestones for implementation of the Controlled Unclassified Information framework. The metric is a YES or NO answer.

5A2: DIB CIKR owners and operators conduct self-assessments of the risk to CIKR information related to critical DIB assets identified by the SSA.	5A2A: DIB owners and operators report they have conducted self-assessments using commonly accepted industry standards, guidelines, and best practices (e.g., International Standards Organization (ISO), Federal Information Processing Standards (FIPS), National Institute of Standards, (NIST) and Service Provider's (SPs)). The outcome metric is the percentage of the total.
	5A2C: DIB owners and operators report mitigation of assessed vulnerability to owner-defined acceptable level of risk. The metric is a YES or NO answer.
5A3: DIB CIKR owners and operators implement awareness training for employees responsible for information protection.	5A3A: DIB owners and operators report percentage of employees responsible for information protection who have received annual security awareness training.
5A4: DIB owners and operators identify and adopt commonly accepted industry standards and government regulations for the protection of information.	5A4A: DIB owners and operators report adoption of industry standards, guidelines, best practices (e.g., ISO, FIPS, NIST, and SPs), and associated information security programs for protection of DoD information. The response is expressed as a percentage.
5A5: DIB owners and operators develop plans to mitigate risks associated with this information.	5A5A: DIB owners and operators report they have risk mitigation plans for high and medium risks identified through their self-assessment processes. The response is expressed as a percentage.
5B1: SSA identifies standards and guidelines for the protection of DIB electronic information and communication systems, networks, and control systems.	5B1B: DoD acquisition and contracting policy includes requirements and guidance for the protection of unclassified DoD information not publicly releasable that resides on or transits DIB unclassified systems or networks. The metric is a YES or NO answer.
5B2: DIB owners and operators apply IA standards and guidelines to mitigate risks to these systems, networks, and control systems commensurate with the level of protection needed for the information at risk.	5B2A: DIB owners and operators report adoption of industry standards, guidelines, best practices (e.g., ISO, FIPS, NIST, SPs), and associated information security programs for the protection of their systems, networks, and control systems. The response is expressed as a percentage.
5B3: DIB owners and operators implement awareness training for employees responsible for these systems, networks, and control systems.	5B3A: DIB owners and operators report implementation of annual security awareness training for employees responsible for systems, networks, and control systems. The response is expressed as a percentage.

5B4: DIB Sector partners develop and implement methodologies for information sharing in a comprehensive, multi-tiered, dynamic, information-sharing network designed to provide timely and actionable threat information, assessments, and warnings to public and private sector partners.

5B4A: DoD partners with DIB members through a framework agreement that initiates unclassified and classified threat information sharing with partners, incident reporting by DIB partners, and collaboration on cyber intrusion damage assessments as needed.

5B4B: Secure electronic means to disseminate classified threat information between DoD and participating DIB partners is established.

5B4C: DIB owners and operators report that information provided by the government is timely and actionable in mitigating risk to DIB systems, networks, and control systems.

The metric for each is a YES or NO answer.

7. CIKR Protection Research and Development

7.1 Overview of Sector R&D

The DIB recognizes that a fully operational R&D plan is instrumental for identification and development of technologies to identify threats, assess risks and vulnerabilities, and enhance the resilience and protective posture for the sector. Since 2007, the DIB has been generating requirements, assessing the processes, and mapping the way toward development of the DIB Sector R&D Plan. The SSA will collaborate with DoD and with other SSAs, and owners and operators to develop a focused DIB Sector program in the near term. This approach will enable identification of areas where R&D would be beneficial, identify and leverage initiatives currently underway, and champion new R&D initiatives that align with the DIB Sector.

The National Critical Infrastructure Protection Research and Development Plan (NCIP R&D Plan) was first developed and approved in 2004 in response to HSPD-7. The plan is a companion document to the NIPP. The national strategies guiding the NCIP R&D Plan include the National Strategy for Homeland Security, National Strategy for the Physical Protection of Critical Infrastructures and Key Assets, and National Strategy to Secure Cyberspace.

Cyber Highlights

The DoD DIB CS/IA program explores technology solutions, network architecture, and related issues to help protect critical unclassified information on DIB systems and networks. This is accomplished in part under the program's working groups.

The DHS Science & Technology Directorate (DHS S&T) is responsible for annual updates to the NCIP R&D Plan, and does so in coordination with the Federal interagency R&D community. DHS coordinates the plan via the Infrastructure Subcommittee (ISC) of the National Science and Technology Council. The plan's primary purpose is to examine all the R&D categories that could enable implementation of the NIPP and enhance infrastructure security and resilience. In addition, it highlights categories that have relevance to multiple sectors.

The NCIP R&D Plan focuses on nine technology themes reflecting the concerns of infrastructure owners/operators, industry representatives, academia, and government officials. Each theme addresses physical and cyber R&D. Rather than each CIKR sector sponsoring projects to address an individual sector need, the goal is to develop common cross-sector solutions that each sector can further customize to meet its specific needs. The nine technology themes are:

- Detection and Sensor Systems;
- Protection and Prevention;
- Entry and Access Portals;

- Insider Threats;

- Analysis and Decision Support Systems;

- Response, Recovery, and Reconstitution;

- New and Emerging Threats and Vulnerabilities;

- Advanced Infrastructure Architectures and Systems Design; and

- Human and Social Issues.

The National CIKR Protection Annual Report (NAR) is based on requirements established in HSPD-7 and the NIPP, with substantive input based on information contained in the SSPs and SARs. The NAR also identifies the R&D agendas developed by the sectors to achieve their goals and objectives, and reports progress in relevant R&D efforts. The agendas focus on operational and shorter term capability gaps to provide affordable, effective solutions and knowledge advancements for meaningful risk reduction. The NCIP R&D Plan examines sector requirements and identifies transformational, longer term research to ensure that fundamental problems and longer term stretch goals are identified, and that the progress made toward meeting them is reported.

The NIPP R&D Requirements Process is the DHS IP and DHS S&T's framework for collecting, validating, and prioritizing CIKR sector requirements and capability gaps, and developing solutions to execute the CIKR protection and resilience mission. DHS released an annual report in September 2008 that documents R&D activity conducted in 2007 and 2008.

The 2008 DIB SAR addressed three key findings reported by the NIPP Requirements Steering Group. The first key finding involved an extensive mapping process. This process showed that most sector-identified capability gaps are being addressed by either existing or planned sector R&D projects within DHS S&T. The second key finding was that CIKR sectors should submit identified capability gaps to the S&T Capstone Integrated Product Team (IPT) process when existing or planned sector R&D projects do not meet stated R&D needs. This S&T R&D planning and execution framework was established in 2007. An extensive outreach effort occurred in late 2007 and early 2008 to ensure that all sectors were fully aware of the R&D opportunities available through the S&T Capstone IPT construct. The third key finding was the need for a more structured R&D reporting process. This issue was the fundamental focus for IP's R&D team for 2007 and early 2008. To begin to address this need, DHS/IP and DHS S&T developed and published the 2008 Sector Annual Report Guidance that included a Capability Gap Statement template for R&D reporting. The template provides a structured approach to articulating CIKR protection needs and demonstrates the maturation of the NIPP R&D process.

DHS S&T established Capstone IPTs to provide DHS customers with R&D solutions to identify capability gaps. The process is set up to encourage direct inputs to the R&D process. Senior leaders from DHS components serve as the chairs for each Capstone IPT and provide key inputs to the S&T R&D process. Capstone IPTs operate at the strategic level and focus on validating and prioritizing capability gaps to help make decisions on funding technical solutions. Funding decisions are inherently governmental and not open to the private sector. Private sector end users, however, may be invited to provide particular expertise at a given Capstone meeting. Once funding decisions are made, project-level IPTs are formed. The project-level IPTs work the solution from cradle to grave and coordinate with the private sector end users to develop details on requirements, deliverables, and acquisition strategies.

The DIB Sector will increase activities in support of OSTP and DHS S&T in developing the NCIP R&D Plan. As the DIB SSA, DoD recognizes the need to develop, manage, and coordinate R&D requirements and activities for the sector. The DIB SCC is committed to its R&D partnership role as an end user, and plans to increase activities in defining sector operational and capability needs and technology gaps. The sector intends to develop an initial DIB Sector R&D Plan in 2011. Development of the R&D plan will enable DoD to better identify its R&D gaps and support the NIPP R&D process.

7.2 Sector R&D Requirements

DIB Sector R&D requirements are generated from information received from DIB owners and operators and other sector partners, generally via the GCC and SCC coupled with threat and risk information. To date, DIB Sector capability gaps have been submitted through the annual reporting process and are included in the DHS R&D Plan:

- Protection and Prevention – "Ensure interoperability with HSIN and DCIP COP"
- Insider Threat Detection
- Entry and Access Portals – "Facilities access and credentialing"

The DIB Sector recognizes the need for and value of R&D to address some of the security-related challenges facing CIKR owners and operators. Owners and operators will continue to explore, test, and utilize technologies and equipment to mitigate risks and threats where appropriate. Of the nine technology themes identified above, the DIB will collaboratively focus primarily on the following: Insider Threats, Technology Transfer, Manmade/Natural Disasters/Continuity of Operations, and Screening and Protection of Employees, Partners and Suppliers. A more structured approach based on the DIB R&D Plan to be developed in 2011 will enhance the sector's ability to identify operational capabilities, determine technology gaps, and prioritize R&D requirements.

7.3 Sector R&D Plan

The DIB Sector plans to establish an ad hoc CIPAC DIB R&D Working Group, with the mission to define and institutionalize the process organizing and analyzing R&D and risk information, and reporting sector operational requirements and capability gaps to DHS. DoD will solicit representatives from policy, R&D, technology, and acquisition management organizations such as OASD (HD&ASA), USD (AT&L), DUSD Industrial Policy, DUSD Science and Technology, Defense Advanced Research Projects (DARPA) Director, Systems and Software Engineering, DCMA, OASD (NII), and the newly formed U.S. Cyber Command. The DIB SCC will provide sector end user CIKR experts. Expert focus areas will include information sharing/management, cybersecurity, people screening, infrastructure protection, preparedness and response: incident management, preparedness and response, and interoperability. This CIPAC DIB R&D ad hoc working group plans to develop and issue the first DIB Sector R&D Plan in 2011.

7.4 R&D Management Process

DoD will leverage the DHS R&D efforts and national technologies, and share those approaches with the DIB CIKR owners and operators and other CIKR partners, as appropriate. DoD will identify technology requirements annually in support of the DIB Sector.

DoD will annually solicit a list of current CIP R&D initiatives from OSTP to evaluate for potential support of DIB requirements. DoD will compile its annual integrated list of technology requirements in support of the DIB and submit R&D requirements through the DHS capability gap statement template.

A number of metrics presented in chapter 6 relate to protection-focused R&D activities to track and measure performance via the DIB Sector metrics reporting process.

DoD and the DIB SCC are fully committed to support the DHS S&T Capstone and project-level IPTs, and will identify a primary point of contact (POC) to ensure proper DIB Sector coordination.

The DIB SCC will provide independent operational capability and technology gap information through the CIKR Cross-Sector Council.

8. Responsibilities

This chapter describes the processes that DoD uses to support its responsibilities as the DIB SSA and how it ensures these responsibilities are carried out. DoD is designated as the SSA for the DIB Sector in HSPD-7, a designation elaborated on in the 2009 NIPP.

In addition, this chapter provides further clarification of the DIB partnership, processes, programs, and tools used to protect and support the CIKR. The DIB Sector has progressed in its relationships with CIKR partners since 2007, with development of the collaborative GCC and SCC goals, objectives, implementation actions, RMAs, and metrics as discussed in chapter 1. The 16 RMAs described in chapter 5 establish individual and shared GCC and SCC responsibilities to build protection and resilience efforts into the DIB sector. Partners continue to build interpersonal and collaborative relationships through these activities as well as establish GCC and SCC working groups, where issues of significance are discussed under the CIPAC umbrella. A key sector issue that stands out is the need for better two-way sharing of information. In FY2009, the DIB GCC established an ISWG to mirror the SCC ISWG. Under the auspices of CIPAC, the GCC and SCC began to formulate information-sharing requirements and will continue into FY2011. By continuing to refine efforts on better information sharing, the partnership will be prepared to address vulnerability, consequences, and impacts that can result in the degradation of an asset. DIB partners will identify solutions to resolve barriers and gaps that negatively influence effective and timely two-way sharing of information.

8.1 DIB SSA Responsibilities

HSPD-7 defines the roles and responsibilities of sector-specific Federal agencies. The following are citations from the directive.

HSPD-7 assigned responsibility for the DIB to DoD.

Paragraph (18)(g) states:

> "Recognizing that each infrastructure sector possesses its own unique characteristics and operating models, there are designated sector-specific agencies, including:
>
> Department of Defense – Defense Industrial Base."

Paragraph (19) describes authorities assigned to the Secretary of Homeland Security, including the following provisions that affect DoD as the DIB SSA:

> "In accordance with guidance provided by the Secretary [DHS], sector-specific agencies shall:
>
> (a) collaborate with all relevant Federal departments and agencies, State and local governments, and the private sector, including with key persons and entities in their infrastructure sector;

(b) conduct or facilitate vulnerability assessments of the sector; and

(c) encourage risk management strategies to protect against and mitigate the effects of attacks against critical infrastructure and key resources."

Paragraph (22) describes roles and responsibilities of other departments, agencies, and offices including the following provisions in which DoD is cited.

"In addition to the responsibilities given the Department and sector-specific agencies, there are special functions of various Federal departments and agencies and components of the Executive Office of the President related to critical infrastructure and key resources protection.

(a) The Department of State, in conjunction with the Department, and the Departments of Justice, Commerce, Defense, the Treasury and other appropriate agencies, will work with foreign countries and international organizations to strengthen the protection of United States critical infrastructure and key resources.

(b) All Federal departments and agencies shall work with the sectors relevant to their responsibilities to reduce the consequences of catastrophic failures not caused by terrorism."

Paragraph (24) describes DoD's responsibilities for its internal infrastructure, which is the focus of the DCIP.

"All Federal department and agency heads are responsible for the identification, prioritization, assessment, remediation, and protection of their respective internal critical infrastructure and key resources. Consistent with the Federal Information Security Management Act of 2002, agencies will identify and provide information security protections commensurate with the risk and magnitude of the harm resulting from the unauthorized access, use, disclosure, disruption, modification, or destruction of information."

Paragraph (25) describes responsibilities for coordination with the private sector.

"In accordance with applicable laws or regulations, the Department and the sector-specific agencies will collaborate with appropriate private sector entities and continue to encourage the development of information sharing and analysis mechanisms. Additionally, the Department and sector-specific agencies shall collaborate with the private sector and continue to support sector-coordinating mechanisms:

(a) to identify, prioritize, and coordinate the protection of critical infrastructure and key resources; and

(b) to facilitate sharing of information about physical and cyber threats, vulnerabilities, incidents, potential protective measures, and best practices."

Paragraph (31) directs the Secretary of Homeland Security to collaborate with DoD and other agencies in implementing the infrastructure protection program.

"The Secretary will collaborate with other appropriate Federal departments and agencies to develop a program, consistent with applicable law, to geospatially map, image, analyze, and sort critical infrastructure and key resources by utilizing commercial satellite and airborne systems, and existing capabilities within other agencies. National technical means should be considered as an option of last resort. The Secretary, with advice from the Director of Central Intelligence, the Secretaries of Defense and the Interior, and the heads of other appropriate Federal departments and agencies, shall develop mechanisms for accomplishing this initiative."

Paragraph (34) describes Federal department responsibilities to plan for protecting physical and cyber critical infrastructure.

"By July 2004, the heads of all Federal departments and agencies shall develop and submit to the Director of the OMB for approval plans for protecting the physical and cyber critical infrastructure and key resources that they own or operate.

These plans shall address identification, prioritization, protection, and contingency planning, including the recovery and reconstitution of essential capabilities."

8.2 DIB Oversight and Coordination

DoD administers its DIB SSA responsibilities through the Deputy ASD (DASD) for Homeland Defense Strategy, Prevention & and Force Planning, and Mission Assurance under the control, authority, and supervision of ASD (HD&ASA). Paragraph 19 of HSPD-7 directs DoD to:

- Collaborate with all relevant Federal departments and agencies, State and local governments, and the private sector, including key people and entities in their infrastructure sectors;

- Conduct or facilitate vulnerability assessments of the DIB Sector; and

- Encourage risk management strategies to protect against and mitigate the effects of attacks against CIKR.

As the DIB SSA, DoD seeks to engage in ongoing activities that:

- Improve trust between the government and DIB owners and operators to support two-way information sharing;

- Maintain meaningful and frequent dialogue across the diverse array of DIB CIKR partners; and

- Reduce the burden of remediating or mitigating vulnerabilities for the highest priority critical DIB assets wherever possible.

The DoD approach to managing CIKR protection is threefold.

- The DASD for Homeland Defense Strategy, Prevention & Force Planning, and Mission Assurance initiates policy approved through the DoD policy coordination process, and establishes strategy and procedures for program implementation.

- The DASD for Homeland Defense Strategy, Prevention & Force Planning, and Mission Assurance collaborates to manage program priorities and respond to industry needs with its DIB government partners through the DIB GCC and with industry through the SCC (see section 1.2). DoD continues to collaborate with DHS, primarily through IP, to conform to national CIKR guidance and coordinate on legislative, policy, and program matters affecting the DIB Sector consistent with Federal laws, regulations, and policies.

- The DASD for Homeland Defense Strategy, Prevention & Force Planning, and Mission Assurance delegates vulnerability and overall risk assessment responsibility to DoD components that have existing DIB responsibilities and expertise. This includes the USD (AT&L), who has overall DoD policy responsibility for the DIB; DCMA, for DIB CIKR assessment management; and the National Guard, for assessment execution.

8.3 Processes and Responsibilities

8.3.1 SSP Maintenance and Update

DoD reviews the SSP annually with its GCC and SCC partners and makes revisions as required in alignment with DHS guidance. The ASD (HD&ASA) leads DIB SSP reviews and updates to the DIB SSP with full participation of the DIB GCC and SCC. Each member signs an acknowledgement letter attesting to its role in reviewing and implementing the SSP.

8.3.2 SSP Implementation Milestones

DoD collaborates with its DIB Sector CIKR partners to acquire the information necessary to prepare the SAR. As operational lead, DCMA works with the DIB GCC and SCC to establish effective information collection mechanisms. DCMA will collect information from owners, operators, and suppliers supported by the DIB SCC where applicable and in conformance with its charter.

8.3.3 Resources and Budgets

DoD has maintained centralized responsibility for building, managing, and tracking the DIB CIP program budget and resources at DoD headquarters level within OASD (HD&ASA). The DIB CS/IA program budget is overseen by the DoD DIB CS/IA program under ASD (NII)/DoD CIO. The Program Office works closely with OASD (HD&ASA) and other DoD components to resource the requirements as the program expands, to include emergent capabilities in the areas of incident analysis and cyber intrusion damage assessment, among others.

The ASD (HD&ASA) uses a strategic and performance management model to meet both DoD internal agency CIP and DIB SSA responsibilities. DoD reviews the DIB mission and vision statements, guiding principles, and organizational values annually, and refines and prioritizes the goals presented in chapter 1 in collaboration with sector partners. DoD builds funding plans to support capabilities required to perform activities and then uses outcome-based metrics to track performance.

In the near term, the ASD (HD&ASA) will continue to manage the policy, oversight, and advocacy elements of the budget, and DCMA will manage the integration and coordination elements to execute SSA executive agent responsibilities. The DIB GCC and SCC will contribute to the development of sector requirements and priorities to inform the resource management process.

8.3.4 Training and Education

DoD understands that a successful DIB risk management effort requires effective training, education, and outreach. DoD seeks to enhance those efforts and support DIB Sector CIKR partners in expanding their education and training programs and initiatives. To communicate the importance of these efforts effectively, DoD will meet with senior executives and managers, intelligence analysts, assessment teams, and security personnel. Current training, education, and outreach programs include:

- **DCIP Awareness Visits:** DoD organizes awareness visits to include representatives from the full spectrum of DIB CIKR partners. The intent of a DCIP awareness visit is to educate the audience, particularly facility security and management personnel and local first responders, regarding DoD CIKR protection and resilience responsibilities and goals.

- **DIB Mission Assurance Assessment Training:** The National Guard Joint Interagency Training Center provides training intended for individuals who perform facility-level assessments.

- **DIB CIP Annual Training Conference:** DoD sponsors a conference to bring together senior DoD officials and DIB asset owners to enhance CIKR protection-related capabilities. The conference includes a series of presentations delivered by DoD leaders, private sector executives, and State, local, and international partners. In addition, a series of subject matter panels and technical breakout working sessions is held.

- **Level I Anti-Terrorism Awareness:** Train individuals on the indicators of terrorism and how to properly report suspicious activities and operational anomalies.

- **Computer Security Awareness:** DoD provides computer security awareness training and annual updates for all DoD service members and civilian employees.

- **Cyber Investigations Training:** The National Defense Authorization Act for FY2010 provides authority for the Secretary of Defense to permit eligible private sector employees to receive instruction at the Defense Cyber Investigations Training Academy operating under the direction of the DoD Cyber Crime Center. This program would provide specialized training in subject areas such as DIB network analysis, reporting response, and collection of data related to cyber intrusions.

8.4 Implementing the Sector Partnership Model

8.4.1 NIPP Coordination Councils

The principal coordinating bodies for the DIB are the DIB GCC and SCC. These bodies act as DIB Sector representatives to the Government Cross-Sector Council and CIKR Cross-Sector Council, respectively, for the DIB and serve as the DIB leadership focal points for national level coordination. See section 1.2 and appendix 5.

CIPAC

CIPAC provides the opportunity for industry and government partners to discuss DIB-related CIP issues, normally in the form of joint GCC and SCC meetings. DHS established the CIPAC as a Federal Advisory Committee Act exempt body, pursuant to the authority provided in 6 U.S.C. 451. Under CIPAC, DIB CIKR partners may engage in a broad range of activities, such as:

- Planning, coordination, implementation, and operational issues;

- Implementation of security programs;

- Operational activities related to CIKR protection and resilience, including incident response, recovery, and reconstitution; and

- Development and support of national plans, including the NIPP and SSPs.

Department of State Overseas Security Advisory Council

DOS coordinate the Overseas Security Advisory Council (OSAC) that provides security information to, and coordinates security issues with, U.S. businesses overseas. DoD, DHS, and DOS coordinate their efforts to reduce duplication of effort and enhance the effectiveness of CIPAC, OSAC, and DoD programs for DIB CIKR protection in the international arena.

8.4.2 Homeland Infrastructure Foundation-Level Database Working Group

The Homeland Infrastructure Foundation-Level Database (HIFLD) Working Group is a coalition of Federal, State, and local government organizations that collaborate with federally funded R&D centers, and supporting private industry partners. Members are Federal entities involved with geospatial or "location awareness" issues related to homeland security, homeland defense, civil support, or emergency preparedness and response. Co-sponsored by OASD (HD&ASA), DHS, the National Geospatial-Intelligence Agency, and the U.S. Geological Survey, the HIFLD Working Group includes representatives from numerous government agencies, including U.S. Northern Command. The group promotes domestic and international infrastructure geospatial information sharing, protection, and knowledge management.

8.4.3 State, Local, Tribal, and Territorial Government Coordinating Council Liaisons

The State, Local, Tribal and Territorial Government Coordinating Council (SLTTGCC) provide liaison representatives who are influential and knowledgeable leaders on CIKR-related issues to the DIB GCC. These liaisons bring a diverse set of State, local, tribal, and territorial government perspectives and interests and assist the DIB SSA and GCC with identifying and developing collaborative strategies that advance CIKR protection and resilience. Membership in the GCC will be expanded to include more representation from across Federal, State, and local governments. These liaisons will continue to be included in the writing and editing of both the SSP and SAR.

8.4.4 International CIKR Partners

The DIB is global in nature and the protection and resilience of all DIB infrastructure is crucial to mission success. DIB assets overseas, similar to U.S. based assets, are unique as they are privately owned and cooperation with the U.S. Government is voluntary. Ensuring the protection and resilience of DIB assets overseas has increasing complications, and the SSA must establish outreach programs with DOS, embassies, and foreign governments, and make regional project arrangements and other agreements before reaching out to an asset. While the SSA has made progress working with DOS and taking steps to establish agreements since the 2007 SSP, reaching out to assets overseas are further complicated by the need to establish information assurance programs to protect sensitive information.

The international DIB community cannot rely on the DIB value proposition that a consensus-driven partnership draws on the active, voluntary, and full engagement of all DIB partners. The DIB Sector must first establish a partnership with the foreign government before reaching out to the DIB partner. As such, the DIB Sector must develop a strategy for building partnership capacity with nations hosting DIB assets.

Outside the United States, DoD works through the COCOMs and DOS via international agreements and other diplomatic channels and processes to ensure the ability of international DIB assets and eliminate unacceptable risk to national security. OASD (HD&ASA) and DCMA work together to institute effective cooperation with international DIB partners and develop protective actions through the sector planning process specified in appendix 1B of the 2009 NIPP and the annual Critical Foreign Dependencies Initiative (CFDI) Action Plans.

DCMA is the DoD agency responsible for executing the DIB SSA responsibilities, and has approximately 10,000 employees in more than 900 locations worldwide. DCMA has an office specifically dedicated to international operations. This capability supports the assessment and risk response aspects of the DIB CIP risk management program. This results in a global DIB CIP effort wherein international critical DIB assets are defined and prioritized, vulnerability assessments are planned, and incident response capabilities are in place to address the impact of actual events.

OASD (HD&ASA) and DCMA work together to implement existing agreements that effect DIB CIKR protection and resilience, as exemplified by ongoing coordination with the Canadian Department of National Defense (DND) as part of the 2005 Security and Prosperity Partnership of North America (SPP) and North American Technology and Industrial Base Organization (NATIBO).

The trilateral SPP was launched in March 2005 to increase security and enhance prosperity among the United States, Canada, and Mexico through greater cooperation and information sharing. The SPP is intended to prevent and respond to threats in North America, including development and implementation of a common approach to critical infrastructure protection in response to cross-border terrorist incidents and natural disasters. The SPP supports developing and implementing compatible protective and response strategies and programs for shared DIB critical infrastructure.

NATIBO facilitates technology and industrial base efforts between the United States and Canada in support of North American security. DCMA, in conjunction with the OASD (HD&ASA), works closely with NATIBO to ensure a cost-effective, healthy technology and industrial base that is responsive to the national and economic security needs of the United States and Canada.

OASD (HD&ASA), USD (AT&L), and DCMA also work closely with their Canadian DND counterparts as part of the DIB Critical Infrastructure Protection Working Group established under NATIBO. This working group seeks to develop and implement a common approach to CIP and cross-border incident response.

The European Command CIP Office supports OASD (HD&ASA) with NATO CIP efforts. The Conference of National Armaments Directors developed a NATO Defense Against Terrorism Programme of Work (DAT POW) as part of an enhanced set of measures to strengthen NATO's fight against terrorism. DAT POW is looking at 11 critical areas focused on technology to help prevent or mitigate the effects of terrorist attacks; one POW is dedicated completely to CIP.

Many of the partners and processes that the DIB relies on are global in nature and may require different approaches to strengthen CIKR protection efforts. This includes multinational partnerships with substantial interdependencies outside the United States. To help ensure that relationships with these international private and public sector partners support effective DIB CIKR strategies, the DIB SSA works with DOS and COCOM CIP liaison officers and other government agencies to:

- Identify and evaluate relevant contracts and Service Level Agreements between foreign suppliers and U.S. entities supporting the DIB.

- Identify existing international agreements and foreign laws that can assist the DIB with its overseas CIKR efforts.

- Work with other sectors and FBI legal attaches to evaluate the actual capacity of relevant foreign governments to address international CIKR issues within their own countries that can affect the DIB.

- Consider joint/multilateral efforts where foreign governments and companies can directly cooperate on risk assessments, threat and hazard monitoring, vulnerability mitigation planning, and international outreach efforts to directly support the DIB.

- Work with the National Guard Bureau to identify existing CIKR training and education materials that can be shared with foreign partners, especially where an international relationship might already exist, and convert them using appropriate translations, locally relevant structure, and culturally appropriate formats to ensure effective communication of dissemination.

8.5 Information Sharing and Reporting

Many organizations have an interest or role in identifying and coordinating the protection and resilience of critical DIB assets. Each organization must clearly understand its individual roles and responsibilities, as well as the roles and responsibilities of other contributing organizations, to ensure there are no gaps in response and there is minimal duplication of effort. In addition, DoD must ensure each organization is furnished with the information necessary to appropriately prevent, plan for, and respond to emerging threats and incidents that are relevant to the DIB Sector.

DoD has identified the venues and mechanisms for sharing information with the various DIB CIP communities of interest. These communities include domestic organizations (including industry); international private industry; international coalitions and allies; Federal, State, and local governments and agencies; and other DoD organizations.

DoD and the SCC employ a variety of forums and mechanisms to share information:

- DIB GCC, SCC, and CIPAC meetings;

- DCIP awareness visits;

- DIBNet-U (unclassified) and DIBNet-S (classified) DoD threat information sharing with DIB CS/IA program partners;

- Industry association meetings and expositions;

- US-CERT DSIE portal as well as DSIE bimonthly meetings;

- JCC pilot program with DSIE and other sector partners;

- PCIS;

- CSCSWG;

- NSIE/DSIE relationships;

- Academic symposia and conferences;

- Electronic and traditional mail; and

- Homeland Security Information Network – Critical Sector (HSIN-CS) and HSIN DIB portals.

Mechanisms for communicating roles, responsibilities, and concepts for effective DIB CIP efforts include:

- US-CERT DSIE portal for sharing cyber attack and mitigation information;

- DIB SSP;

- Published policy, directives, instructions, guidance, and methodology;

- Documented concept of operations;

- Presentations and speaking engagements at association, international, Federal, State, and local events, expositions, and conferences;

- Participation in exercises and published lessons learned; and

- Onsite awareness presentations at DIB sites and curricula at Defense Acquisition University and other schools, such as the Homeland Security Centers of Excellence, which are authorized by law and chosen by DoD's Science and Technology Directorate through a competitive selection process.

The most significant challenge for DoD in working with DIB CIKR is establishing trusted relationships where the private sector is assured the government can and will protect its business-sensitive, proprietary, and confidential information from public disclosure and misuse. As a first step in establishing that trust, DoD became an accredited partner in the PCII program. The program is an information sharing/protection program through which the private sector may voluntarily share homeland security-related CII with the Federal Government in a protected manner. In turn, the private sector is assured the information it provides will be exempt from public disclosure, and will be used only by authorized personnel with appropriate PCII training and certification.

Recognizing that the preponderance of the critical infrastructure upon which our national security, economy, and public welfare depend is owned and operated by the private sector, Congress passed the Critical Infrastructure Information Act of 2002 (CII Act) to encourage private sector information sharing by providing distinct protections for voluntarily shared CII.

Information, if it meets the requirements of the CII Act, is protected from:

- Disclosure under the Freedom of Information Act;

- Disclosure under similar State and local laws;

- Use in civil litigation; and

- Use in regulatory proceedings.

As an accredited partner in the PCII program, DoD has established the PCII Program Office as the sole office authorized to implement, manage, and oversee DoD's PCII activity. The program office facilitates access to PCII, coordinates required training, and provides operating procedures for all aspects of care and use of PCII. The PCII program ensures compliance with the governing authorities and is based in DCIP, ASD (HD&ASA). The PCII Program Officer is responsible for strict adherence to safeguarding, handling, use, and storage of PCII by DoD personnel, and for establishing a self-inspection program that includes periodic review and assessment of compliance in the handling, use, and storage of PCII.

The DoD PCII program facilitates access to PCII, not previously available to DoD components, in two ways:

- Obtaining and maintaining accreditation status, the DoD PCII program has demonstrated that it meets and deploys rigorous standards for the use and handling of PCII to safeguard its proprietary and business-sensitive information from public disclosure and misuse.

- Developing special arrangements with DHS to allow private sector CII to be given directly to DoD components for immediate use and which is fully protected upon receipt.

Some DCIP DIB information requires security classification. In these instances, DoD will continue to classify information according to applicable regulations, and will follow classified networks and systems accreditation processes for information-sharing needs. There is a possibility that DCIP DIB information will have a security classification and PCII status. In all instances, all DCIP DIB information will be protected to the fullest extent, and will be handled only by appropriate personnel who are trained and who have a need to know that information.

In accordance with applicable laws or regulations, OASD (HD&ASA) and DoD components will collaborate with appropriate private sector entities and continue to encourage development of information-sharing and analysis mechanisms. In addition, DoD and other HSPD-7 SSAs will collaborate with the private sector and continue to support sector coordinating mechanisms.

DoD will continue to develop information-sharing policy, processes, and procedures to enhance two-way communication between DoD and DIB asset owners, building on the success of the DoD DIB CS/IA pilot program and establishment of the GCC and SCC. DoD and the asset owners must continue to build trusted relationships and work collaboratively to protect DoD and DIB assets. In addition, the DIB CS/IA program has become an information-sharing model for other NIPP sectors.

Appendix 1: Glossary

All Hazards. A grouping classification encompassing all conditions, environmental or manmade, that have the potential to cause injury, illness, or death; damage to or loss of equipment, infrastructure services, or property; or alternatively causing functional degradation to social, economic, or environmental aspects.

Asset (Infrastructure). A distinguishable network entity that provides a service or capability. Assets are people, physical entities, or information located either within or outside the United States and owned or operated by domestic, foreign, public, or private sector organizations. DHS states an asset is a person, structure, facility, information, material, or process that has value. In the context of the NIPP, people are not considered assets.

Business Continuity. Strategic and tactical capability of the organization to plan for and respond to incidents and business disruptions and continue business operations at an acceptable predefined level. DHS states business continuity is the ability of an organization to continue to function before, during, and after a disaster.

CIKR Partner. Those Federal, State, regional, local, tribal, or territorial government entities, public and private sector owners and operators and representative organizations, regional organizations and coalitions, academic and professional entities, and certain not-for-profit and private volunteer organizations that share in the responsibility for protecting the Nation's CIKR.

Consequence. The effect of an event, incident, or occurrence. For the purposes of the NIPP, consequences are divided into four main categories: public health and safety, economic, psychological, and governance impacts.

Control Systems. Computer-based systems used within many infrastructures and industries to monitor and control sensitive processes and physical functions. These systems typically collect measurement and operational data from the field, process and display the information, and relay control commands to local or remote equipment or human-machine interfaces (operators). Examples of types of control systems include Supervisory Control and Data Acquisition systems, Process Control Systems, and Distributed Control Systems.

Critical Infrastructure. Systems and assets, whether physical or virtual, so vital that the incapacity or destruction of them may have a debilitating impact on the security, economy, public health or safety, environment, or any combination of these factors, across any Federal, State, regional, territorial, or local jurisdiction.

Critical Infrastructure Information (CII). Information that is not customarily in the public domain and is related to the security of critical infrastructure or protected systems. CII consists of records and information concerning any of the following:

- Actual, potential, or threatened interference with, attack on, compromise of, or incapacitation of critical infrastructure or protected systems by either physical or computer-based attack or other similar conduct (including the misuse of or unauthorized access to all types of communications and data transmission systems) that violates Federal, State, or local law; harms the interstate commerce of the United States; or threatens public health or safety.

- The ability of any critical infrastructure or protected system to resist such interference, compromise, or incapacitation, including any planned or past assessment, projection, or estimate of the vulnerability of critical infrastructure or a protected system, including security testing, risk evaluation thereto, risk management planning, or risk audit.

- Any planned or past operational problem or solution regarding critical infrastructure or protected systems, including repair, recovery, insurance, or continuity, to the extent that it is related to such interference, compromise, or incapacitation.

Cybersecurity. The prevention of damage to, unauthorized use of, or exploitation of, and, if needed, the restoration of electronic information and communication systems and the information contained therein to ensure confidentiality, integrity, and availability. Includes protection and restoration, when needed, of information networks and wire line, wireless, satellite, public safety answering points, and 911 communication systems and control systems.

Defense Critical Asset. An asset of such extraordinary importance to DoD operations in peace, crisis, and war that its incapacitation or destruction would have a very serious, debilitating effect on the ability of DoD to fulfill its mission.

Defense Production Act of 1950 (DPA). Under Title I of the act, as amended (50 U.S.C. App. 2061 et seq.), the President is authorized to require preferential acceptance and performance of contracts or orders supporting certain approved national defense and energy programs, and to allocate materials, services, and facilities in such a manner as to promote these approved programs. Under Title VII, the President is authorized to conduct mandatory surveys and analyses, and prepares reports on specific subsectors of the U.S. DIB. The DPA's current definition of "national defense" includes programs for military and energy production or construction, military or critical infrastructure assistance to any foreign nation, homeland security, stockpiling, space, and any directly related activity. The DPA authority has also been extended to support emergency preparedness activities under Title VI of the Robert T. Stafford Disaster Relief and Emergency Assistance Act (the Stafford Act), as amended (42 U.S.C. 5195 et seq.), and critical infrastructure protection and restoration (Public Law 111-67).

Dependency. The one-directional reliance of an asset, system, network, or collection thereof, within or across sectors, on input, interaction, or other requirement from other sources in order to function properly. A relationship or connection whereby one entity is influenced or controlled by another entity. (DoDD 3020.40, 19 Aug 2005)

- **Interdependency.** Relationships or connections between entities of different functions, networks, sectors, or service. (DoDD 3020.40, 19 Aug 2005)

- **Intra-dependency.** Relationships or connections between entities within a common function, network, sector, or service. (DoDD 3020.40, 19 Aug 2005)

DIB Critical Asset. An asset determined by DoD to be critical to successful execution of its missions.

Government Coordinating Council (GCC). The government counterpart to the SCC for each sector established to enable interagency coordination. The GCC is comprised of representatives across various levels of government (Federal, State, local, tribal, and territorial) as appropriate to the security and operational landscape of each individual sector.

Incident. An occurrence, caused by either human action or natural phenomena that require action to prevent or minimize loss of life or damage to property and/or natural resources. (JP 3-28)

Infrastructure. (1) The framework of networked assets that comprise identifiable industries, institutions, or distribution capabilities that enable continued flow of goods and services. (DoDD 3020.40) All building and permanent installations necessary for support, redeployment, and military forces operations (e.g., barracks, headquarters, airfields, communications, facilities, stores, port installations, and maintenance stations) (JP 3-35) (2) The framework of interdependent networks and systems comprising identifiable industries, institutions (including people and procedures), and distribution capabilities that provide a reliable flow of products and services essential to the defense and economic security of the United States, the smooth functioning of government at all levels, and society as a whole. Consistent with the definition in the Homeland Security Act of 2002, infrastructure includes physical, cyber, and/or human elements.

Key Resources. Publicly or privately controlled resources essential to the minimal operation of the economy and government.

Mitigation. Actions taken in response to a warning or after an incident occurs that are intended to lessen the potentially adverse effects on a given military operation or infrastructure. (DoDD 3020.40)

Network. A group or system of interconnected or cooperating entities, normally characterized as being nodes (assets), and the connections that link them. (DoDD 3020.40) The DHS definition of network is a group of components that share information or interact with each other in order to perform a function.

Owners and Operators. Those entities responsible for day-to-day operation and investment in a particular asset or system.

Preparedness. Activities necessary to build, sustain, and improve readiness capabilities to prevent, protect against, respond to, and recover from natural or manmade incidents. Preparedness is a continuous process involving efforts at all levels of government, and between government and the private sector and nongovernmental organizations to identify threats, determine vulnerabilities, and identify required resources to prevent, respond to, and recover from major incidents.

Prevention. The security procedures undertaken by the public and private sectors to discourage terrorist acts. (JP 3-07.2)

Prioritization. In the context of the NIPP, prioritization is the process of using risk assessment results to identify where risk-reduction or mitigation efforts are most needed, and subsequently determine which protective actions should be instituted in order to have the greatest effect.

Protection. Preservation of the effectiveness and survivability of mission-related military and nonmilitary personnel, equipment, facilities, information, and infrastructure deployed or located within or outside the boundaries of a given operational area. (JP 3-0) DHS states that protection is an action or measure taken to cover or shield from exposure, injury, or destruction. In the context of the NIPP, protection includes actions to deter the threat, mitigate the vulnerabilities, or minimize the consequences associated with a terrorist attack or other incident. Protection can included a wide range of activities, such as hardening facilities, building resilience and redundancy, incorporating hazard resistance into facility design, initiating active or passive countermeasures, installing security systems, promoting workforce surety, training and exercises, and implementing cybersecurity measures, among various others.

Recovery Time Objective. Target time set for resumption of product, service, or activity delivery after an incident. NOTE: The recovery time objective must be less than the maximum tolerable period of disruption.

Resilience/resiliency. The adaptive capacity of an organization in a complex and changing environment. (ISO 31000)

NOTE 1: Resilience is the ability of an organization to resist being affected by an event or the ability to return to an acceptable level of performance in an acceptable period after being affected.

NOTE 2: Resilience is the capability of a system to maintain its functions and structure in the face of internal and external change, and to degrade gracefully when it must.

NOTE 3: There are three levels of resilience: National, Continuous Integration (CI System), and Individual.
   A) National—Willpower to bounce back
   B) CI Systems—Identify critical nodes for protection and planning prioritization; create adaptive grids to ensure redundancy
   C) Individual

Response. Activities that address the short-term, direct effects of an incident, including immediate actions to save lives, protect property, and meet basic human needs. Response also includes the execution of emergency operations plans and incident mitigation activities designed to limit the loss of life, personal injury, property damage, and other unfavorable outcomes. As indicated by the situation, response activities include applying intelligence and other information to lessen the effects or consequences of an incident; increasing security operations; continuing investigations into the nature and source of the threat;

---

ongoing surveillance and testing processes; immunizations, isolation, or quarantine; and specific law enforcement operations aimed at preempting, interdicting, or disrupting illegal activity and apprehending actual perpetrators and bringing them to justice.

Risk. Probability and severity of loss linked to threats or hazards. (DoDD 3020.40) DHS states risk is the potential for an unwanted outcome resulting from an incident, event, or occurrence, as determined by its likelihood and the associated consequences.

Risk Management Framework. A planning methodology that outlines the process for setting goals and objectives; identifying assets, systems, and networks; assessing risks; prioritizing and implementing protection programs and resilience strategies; measuring performance; and taking corrective action. Public and private sector entities often include risk management frameworks in their business continuity plans.

Sector. A logical collection of assets, systems, or networks that provide a common function to the economy, government, or society. The NIPP addresses 18 CIKR sectors, identified by the criteria set forth in HSPD-7.

Sector Annual Report (SAR). Sector Annual Reports are due to DHS on or before June 1 of each year.

Sector Coordinating Council (SCC). Self-organized, self-run, and self-governed organizations that are representative of a spectrum of key stakeholders within a sector. SCCs serve as the government's principal point of entry into each infrastructure sector for developing and coordinating a wide range of CIKR protection activities and issues.

Sector Partnership Model. The framework used to promote and facilitate sector and cross-sector planning, coordination, collaboration, and information sharing for CIKR protection involving all levels of government and private sector entities.

Sector-Specific Agency (SSA). Federal departments and agencies identified in HSPD-7 as responsible for coordinating CIKR protection activities in specified CIKR sectors.

Sector-Specific Plan (SSP). Augmenting plans that complement and extend the NIPP and detail the application of the NIPP framework specific to each CIKR sector. SSAs develop SSPs in close collaboration with other sector partners.

System. A functionally, physically, and/or behaviorally related group of regularly interacting or interdependent elements; that group of elements forming a unified whole. (JP 3-0) DHS states a system is a any combination of facilities, equipment, personnel, procedures, and communications integrated for a specific purpose.

Terrorism. The calculated use of unlawful violence or threat of unlawful violence to inculcate fear; intended to coerce or intimidate governments or societies in the pursuit of goals that are generally political, religious, or ideological. (JP 3-07.2)

Threat. An adversary having the intent, capability, and opportunity to cause loss or damage. (DoDD 3020.40) DHS definition of threat is a natural or manmade occurrence, individual, entity, or action that has or indicates the potential to harm life, information, operations, the environment, and/or property.

Value Proposition. A statement that outlines the national and homeland security interest in protecting the Nation's CIKR and articulates benefits gained by all partners through the risk management framework and public-private partnership described in the NIPP.

Vulnerability. The characteristic of an installation, system, asset, application, or its dependencies that could cause it to suffer a degradation or loss (incapacity to perform its designated function) as a result of having been subjected to a certain level of threat or hazard. (DoDD 3020.40) The DHS definition of vulnerability is a physical feature or operational attribute that renders an entity open to exploitation or susceptible to a given hazard.

Appendix 2: List of Acronyms and Abbreviations

ADMIE	Aerospace and Defence Manufacturers' Information Exchange
AIA	Aerospace Industries Association
APM	Asset Prioritization Model
ASD (HD&ASA)	Assistant Secretary of Defense for Homeland Defense & Americas' Security Affairs
ASD (NII)	Assistant Secretary of Defense for Networks and Information Integration
ASIS	American Society of Industrial Security
BIS	Bureau of Industry and Security
CFIUS	Committee on Foreign Investment in the United States
CII	Critical Infrastructure Information
CIKR	Critical Infrastructure and Key Resources
CIP	Critical Infrastructure Protection
CIPAC	Critical Infrastructure Partnership Advisory Council
COI	Community of Interest
CS/IA	Cybersecurity/Information Assurance
DCIP	Defense Critical Infrastructure Program
DCISE	DoD-DIB Collaborative Information Sharing Environment
DC3	DoD Cyber Crime Center
DCMA	Defense Contract Management Agency
DEPSECDEF	Deputy Secretary of Defense
DHS	Department of Homeland Security
DIB	Defense Industrial Base
DJIOC	Defense Joint Intelligence Operations Center
DND	Department of National Defense of Canada
DOC	Department of Commerce
DoD	Department of Defense

DoDD	Department of Defense Directive
DoDI	Department of Defense Instruction
DOS	Department of State
DPAS	Defense Priorities and Allocations System
DSIE	Defense Security Information Exchange
FBI	Federal Bureau of Investigation
FEMA	Federal Emergency Management Agency
FOIA	Freedom of Information Act
GCC	Government Coordinating Council
GIG	Global Information Grid
HITRAC	Homeland Infrastructure Threat and Risk Analysis Center
HSIN-CS	Homeland Security Information Network for Critical Sectors
HSPD	Homeland Security Presidential Directive
IA	Information Assurance
IP	Office of Infrastructure Protection (Division of DHS National Protection and Programs Directorate)
ISWG	Information Sharing Working Group
IT	Information Technology
MOU	Memorandum of Understanding
NATIBO	North American Technology Industrial Base Organization
NCIP	National Critical Infrastructure Protection
NCMS	National Classification Management Society
NDIA	National Defense Industrial Association
NIPP	National Infrastructure Protection Plan
NMCC	National Military Command Center
NMS	National Military Strategy
NNSA	National Nuclear Security Administration
ODNI	Office of the Director of National Intelligence
PCII	Protected Critical Infrastructure Information
R&D	Research and Development
S&T	Science and Technology (DHS Directorate)
SCC	Sector Coordinating Council
SECDEF	Secretary of Defense
SPP	Security and Prosperity Partnership of North America
SSA	Sector-Specific Agency
SSP	Sector-Specific Plan

TSA	Transportation Security Administration
USCG	U.S. Coast Guard
USD (AT&L)	Under Secretary of Defense for Acquisition, Technology, and Logistics
USD (I)	Under Secretary of Defense for Intelligence
USD (P&R)	Under Secretary of Defense for Personnel and Readiness
USGS	U.S. Geological Survey

Appendix 3: References

Statutes

1. Public Law 107-296: Critical Infrastructure Information Act of 2002 (Title II, Subtitle B of the Homeland Security Act of 2002), **http://policy.defense.gov/sections/policy_offices/hd/offices/dcip/pcii/resources.html**

2. 5 U.S.C. 552: The Freedom of Information Act, as amended 2002, **www.usdoj.gov/oip/foia_updates/Vol_XVII_4/page2.htm.**

3. Public Law 107-56, Uniting and Strengthening America by Providing Appropriate Tools Required to Intercept and Obstruct Terrorism Act (USA PATRIOT Act) of 2001, **http://www.gpo.gov/fdsys/pkg/PLAW-107publ56/content-detail.html**

4. 15 U.S.C. App. 2061 et seq., Public Law 111-67, Defense Production Act of 1950, as amended, **http://www.fema.gov/library/viewRecord.do?id=3590**

5. 42 U.S.C. 5121 et seq., The Robert T. Stafford Disaster Relief and Emergency Assistance Act, as amended, **www.dem.dcc.state.nc.us/mitigation/Library/Stafford.pdf, http://www.fema.gov/pdf/about/stafford_act.pdf**

National Strategies

6. The National Strategy for Homeland Security, Homeland Security Council , October 2007, **http://georgewbush-whitehouse.archives.gov/infocus/homeland/nshs/2007/index.html http://www.dhs.gov/xlibrary/assets/nat_strat_homelandsecurity_2007.pdf**

7. The National Security Strategy of the United States, White House, March 16, 2006, **http://georgewbush-whitehouse.archives.gov/nsc/nss/2006/nss2006.pdf**

8. National Strategy for Physical Protection of Critical Infrastructure and Key Assets, White House, February 2003, **www.dhs.gov/xlibrary/assets/Physical_Strategy.pdf**

9. 2010 Quadrennial Homeland Security Review, **http://www.dhs.gov/xlibrary/assets/qhsr_report.pdf**

Homeland Security Presidential Directives

10. HSPD-7, Critical Infrastructure Identification, Prioritization, and Protection, White House, December 17, 2003, **http://www.gpoaccess.gov/wcomp/v39no51.html http://www.dhs.gov/xabout/laws/gc_1214597989952.shtm**

11. HSPD-8, National Preparedness, White House, December 17, 2003, **http://www.dhs.gov/xabout/laws/gc_1199894121015.shtm http://www.gpoaccess.gov/wcomp/v39no51.html**

12. HSPD-23 (Classified)

13. NSPD-54 Cyber Security and Monitoring, White House release on Comprehensive National Cybersecurity Initiative, March 2, 2010

14. Comprehensive National Cybersecurity Initiative
    http://www.whitehouse.gov/cybersecurity/comprehensive-national-cybersecurity-initiative

Executive Plans and Orders

15. National Infrastructure Protection Plan, Department of Homeland Security, January 2009,
    www.dhs.gov/xlibrary/assets/NIPP_Plan.pdf

16. Executive Order 13228, Establishing the Office of Homeland Security and the
    Homeland Security Council, White House, October 8, 2001, as amended,
    http://frwebgate.access.gpo.gov/cgi-bin/getdoc?dbname=2001_register&docid=fr10oc01-144.pdf

17. Executive Order 12919: Under Executive Order 12919, National Defense Industrial Resource Preparedness, June 7, 1994, as amended, the President delegated DPA Title I priorities and allocations authority to the following agency heads: the Secretary of Agriculture with respect to food resources, food resource facilities, and the domestic distribution of farm equipment and commercial fertilizer; the Secretary of Energy with respect to all forms of energy; the Secretary of Health and Human Services with respect to health resources; the Secretary of Transportation with respect to all forms of civil transportation; the Secretary of Defense with respect to water resources; and the Secretary of Commerce for all other materials, services, and facilities, including construction materials (i.e., "industrial resources").
    http://www.archives.gov/federal-register/executive-orders/pdf/12919.pdf

18. Executive Order 12656: Under Executive Order 12656, Assignment of Emergency Preparedness Responsibilities, November 23, 1988, as amended, the President delegated DPA Title VII mandatory authority to conduct surveys and analyses of the U.S. defense industrial base to the Department of Commerce.
    http://www.archives.gov/federal-register/codification/executive-order/12656.html

Department of Defense Issuances and Strategies

19. DoDD 3020.40, DoD Policy and Responsibilities for Critical Infrastructure (DCIP), January 14, 2010, h,
    http://www.dtic.mil/whs/directives

20. DoDD 5144.1, Assistant Secretary of Defense for Networks and Information Integration/DoD Chief Information Officer (ASD (NII)/DoD CIO), May 5, 2005, **http://www.dtic.mil/whs/directives**

21. DoDD 5200.2, DoD Personnel Security Program, April 9, 1999, **http://www.dtic.mil/whs/directives**

22. DoDD 5220.22, National Industrial Security Program, September 27, 2004, **http://www.dtic.mil/whs/directives**

23. DoD Directive 5505. 13E, "DoD Executive Agent (EA) for the DoD Cyber Crime Center (DC3)," March 1, 2010,
    http://www.dtic.mil/whs/directives

24. DoD Instruction 5205.13, "Defense Industrial Base (DIB) Cyber Security/Information Assurance (CS/IA) Activities," January 29, 2010

25. Defense Critical Infrastructure Program Security Classification Guide, **http://www.dtic.mil/whs/directives**

26. The National Defense Strategy of the United States of America, Department of Defense,
    http://www.defense.gov/pubs/2008NationalDefenseStrategy.pdf

27. The National Military Strategy of the United States of America: A Strategy for Today, A Vision for Tomorrow, Joint Chiefs of Staff, 2004, **http://www.defense.gov/news/Mar2005/d20050318nms.pdf**

28. Strategy for Homeland Defense and Civil Support, Department of Defense, June 2005, **http://www.defense.gov/news/Jun2005/d20050630homeland.pdf**

Guidance and Regulation

29. National Preparedness Guidance, Department of Homeland Security, April 27, 2005, **http://www.scd.hawaii.gov/grant_docs/National_Preparedness_Guidance_Apr_27.pdf**

30. Federal Acquisition Regulations (Combination of DoD, General Services Administration, and National Aeronautics and Space Administration, re-issued March 2005), **https://www.acquisition.gov/far/index.html**

31. Defense Federal Acquisition Regulations (Defense Procurement and Acquisition Policy, re-issued), **http://www.acq.osd.mil/dpap/dars/dfarspgi/current/index.html**

32. Defense Priorities and Allocations System, 15 C.F.R. Part 700, Defense Priorities and Allocations System, 15 C.F.R. Part 700, **http://ecfr.gpoaccess.gov/cgi/t/text/textidx?c=ecfr&sid=9fd483a94b1502fcacfdcdbb6e92aad5&rgn=div5&view=text& node=15:2.1.3.2.1&idno=15#15:2.1.3.2.1.12.1.4**

33. National Plan for Research and Development in Support of Critical Infrastructure Protection, Executive Office of the President, Office of Science and Technology Policy; Department of Homeland Security, Science and Technology Directorate, 2004, **http://www.ornl.gov/sci/oetd/documents/ST_2004_NCIP_RD_PlanFINALApr05.pdf**

Charters

34. North American Technology and Industrial Base Charter of 1997, **www.acq.osd.mil/ott/natibo/charter.html**

35. Security and Prosperity Partnership of North America, White House, March 23, 2005, **http://www.spp.gov/**

36. DIB GCC Charter, October 24, 2006 signed by the Defense Critical Infrastructure Office

37. DIB SCC Charter, July 17, 2007 signed by the Sector Coordinating Council

Appendix 4: Cybersecurity/ Information Assurance

CS/IA is arguably the most important and urgent infrastructure protection issue facing the Nation. CS/IA continues to be a DIB Sector priority.

The DIB SSA continues to address risks associated with dependence on IT. The SSA developed and implemented a shared data environment and associated Web services, including activities for the DCIP common operating picture through visualization of assets via the Knowledge Display and Aggregation System/Palenterra. Related activities include leveraging enhancement tools that facilitate information sharing; using the Electronic Portfolio for DIB critical assets, which provides information to DoD senior leaders to support risk management investment decisions; and other analytical systems to provide predictive analysis that enables its user community to avert risk and enhance acquisition, technology, readiness, and operational decisions relevant to the DIB.

With significant disruptions and increasingly sophisticated cyber threats on the rise, collaboration between the Federal Government and DIB owners and operators is a priority, especially to enhance cybersecurity awareness and protection measures that will ensure robust measures to withstand attacks and mitigate risk, and improve resilience to sustain critical operations, respond, and recover within a recovery time objective. Protection planning will involve consideration for cyber elements that support CIKR operations. The DIB Sector has made significant progress and will continue to work aggressively through 2011.

Several significant initiatives are underway to address the cyber threat.

- In May 2010, the Secretary of Defense established U.S. Cyber Command a new subordinate unified command under the U.S. Strategic Command to provide a strategic capability to confront effectively cyber threats to our national and economic security and defend and protect DoD networks. DoD components and DIB members will benefit from implementation of new strategic cybersecurity initiatives in 2010–2011.

- Since 2007, when the Deputy Secretary of Defense directed the ASD (NII)/DoD CIO to establish the DoD DIB CS/IA Program, DoD and the DIB have grown a solid partnership with the common goal of protecting DoD information. The DoD DIB CS/IA program office oversees efforts to secure critical programs and technology by protecting sensitive unclassified DoD information that resides on or transits non-DoD DIB unclassified networks. Protection results from collaboration with DoD components, the private sector, DIB partners, and other Federal departments and agencies. This is accomplished in part through the development, implementation, and execution of policies, processes, and procedures. The means for achieving this is the DCISE under the DoD Cyber Crime Center, which serves as the cybersecurity operational focal point within DoD for interactions with DIB partner signatories of a DoD company bilateral framework agreement.

- Through voluntary agreements with eligible CDCs, the DoD CS/IA program office maintains trusted relationships and secure mechanisms for sharing cyber threat information. DIB cyber incident reporting and cyber intrusion damage assessment is a non-attributed secure process. Under the CS/IA program, DoD operates a scalable Unclassified DIBNet (DIBNet-U) and a DIBNet-S, a secure, certified, and accredited network for information sharing up to SECRET between DoD and participating CDCs (DIB partners).

- In 2010–2011, the focus of this effort will be the continuing expansion of the DIB CS/IA program and expansion of the secure DoD-DIB network (DIBNet).

Industry partners from the DIB private sector established DSIE to share information in a trusted relationship that protects CIKR.

DSIE has signed an agreement with ADMIE in the United Kingdom, and will begin sharing cyber threat information with the Ministry of Defence.

DoD is resolved to secure cyberspace and set conditions for long-term success to shape the future environment and address new threats. As a full partner in the Comprehensive National Cybersecurity Initiative (CNCI) with responsibility for the defense of military networks, DoD will influence the national cyber infrastructure through partnership with the private sector's R&D efforts so that critical national interests are protected from catastrophic damage. Techniques will exploit existing R&D activities and pursue new approaches to develop changing cyber technologies. DoD's enhancement of cybersecurity will be through high-risk/high-return R&D and will identify strategic DoD cyber Science & Technology actions that reduce vulnerabilities and mitigate consequences.

The DHS CSCWG is a forum for sharing information and expertise on wide-ranging cybersecurity issues, and provides awareness, support, and recommendations. Cross-sector issues focused on include opportunities to improve sector coordination around cybersecurity issues and implications of cross-sector cyber dependencies and interdependencies. CSCWG serves as a conduit for sharing cyber information among sectors via the SCC, GCC, SSA, and ISACs.

The DIB SCC has adopted DSIE, a signatory of the SCC, as its Information/Cyber Security Standing Committee. DSIE uses the U.S. CERT portal to exchange cyber threat and warning information. The current membership consists of 35 companies, with more than 156 individuals that signed an NDA to share information via the U.S. CERT portal. DSIE has enabled industry partners to quickly alert others of any ongoing incident and share mitigation strategies for protection of the DoD critical information under their control. Future actions include standards in the cybersecurity area for unclassified information systems, personnel screening, and physical security.

Appendix 5: Other Government Agencies and DIB CIKR Partners

Department of Defense

HSPD-7 assigns to the Secretary of Defense (SecDef) the responsibility for collaborating with relevant partners, encouraging or conducting vulnerability assessments, and encouraging risk management practices for DIB CIKR. DoD organized a council of government officials to represent the major DIB partnership interests of the Federal Government. NDIA organized a council of private sector defense industry officials to represent the voluntary and major partnership interests of the DIB.

Assistant Secretary of Defense for Homeland Defense & Americas' Security Affairs (ASD (HD&ASA))

ASD (HD&ASA) serves the SecDef as the lead SSA official for the DIB commensurate with responsibilities assigned to DoD by HSPD-7. The ASD (HD&ASA) also is responsible for coordinating protection of the Department's critical infrastructure and for DoD participation in the CIP programs at the national, State, and local levels. The ASD (HD&ASA) assigned DIB SSA responsibilities to the Director for CIP under the Deputy Assistant Secretary of Defense for Homeland Defense Strategy, Prevention & and Force Planning, and Mission Assurance.

Under Secretary of Defense for Acquisition, Technology, and Logistics (USD (AT&L))

USD (AT&L) is the Principal Staff Assistant and advisor to SecDef for all matters relating to the Defense Acquisition System. In addition, USD (AT&L) is the lead for developing industrial and technology base assessments and establishing policies to maintain the capability of the DIB to meet DoD needs, a responsibility that overlaps with DIB SSA responsibilities. Because of this overlap, USD (AT&L) has a primary role and contributes to the execution of DIB SSA responsibilities.

Defense Contract Management Agency (DCMA)

ASD (HD&ASA) has assigned DCMA as the operational lead for executing SSA responsibilities because of its established working relationship with DIB owners and operators. DCMA responsibilities are to plan and coordinate with all DoD components and private sector partners that own or operate elements of the DIB to identify, analyze, and assess DIB critical assets and related impacts.

Assistant Secretary of Defense for Networks and Information Integration/DoD Chief Information Officer (ASD (NII)/DoD CIO))

ASD (NII)/DoD CIO serves as the primary advisor to the SecDef for information assurance, networks, network-centric policies and concepts, and DoD enterprise-wide architectures and IT. It is responsible for formulating and implementing enterprise-level network defense strategies including assuring availability of the Global Information Grid (GIG). It oversees DIB CS/IA activities, including related DoD Cyber Crime Center (DC3) activities and chairs the DIB CS/IA Executive Committee. The ASD (NII)/DoD CIO coordinates with USD (AT&L) on the incorporation of DIB CS/IA requirements in acquisition programs, contracts, and regulations, and on cyber intrusion damage assessment matters pertaining to the DIB; coordinates with USD (I) on intelligence, counterintelligence, security support, and the implementation of information security policy as it relates to DIB CS/IA activities and as it relates to adherence to the NISP; coordinate with USD (P) on integrating DIB CS/IA cyber threat information-sharing activities and enhancing DoD and DIB cyber situational awareness in accordance with NSPD-54/HSPD-23 and DoDI 5205.13.

Under Secretary of Defense (Intelligence) (USD (I))

USD (I) is the DoD Senior Security Official responsible for the integration of risk-managed security and protection policies and programs for personnel, physical, industrial, information, operations, chemical/biological, and DoD special access program security, as well as research and technology protection.

Under Secretary of Defense (Personnel and Readiness) (USD (P&R))

USD (P&R) is the principal advisor to SecDef regarding oversight and measurement of readiness to ensure that military forces can execute the National Military Strategy (NMS). The P&R staff oversees development and implementation of the Defense Readiness Reporting System. When fully implemented, the system will integrate information regarding the elements of the DIB. This integration will permit improved assessments of the DIB's ability to deliver required products and services to support DoD mission execution.

Other Federal Departments and Agencies

DoD collaborates with DHS and other SSAs and Federal agencies to ensure the DIB SSP is consistent with and fully supports national critical infrastructure protection efforts. The supporting roles of other Federal departments and agencies include:

DHS, Office of Infrastructure Protection (IP)

- Maintain awareness of critical DIB assets;
- Oversee consistent use of SSA plan guidance across Federal departments and agencies;
- Collaborate with DoD to deter, prevent, and defeat physical and cyber incidents perpetrated against the DIB;
- Collaborate with DoD to conduct or facilitate vulnerability assessments of the DIB;
- Collaborate with DoD to coordinate development of risk management strategies to protect against and mitigate the effects of attacks against the DIB; and
- Collaborate with DoD to identify and establish additional DIB-coordinating mechanisms that identify, prioritize, and coordinate protection of CIKR; and facilitate sharing of information about physical and cyber threats, vulnerabilities, incidents, potential protective measures, and best practices.

DHS, Office of Cyber Security and Communications (CS&C)

The CS&C office, together with IP, is responsible for leading and coordinating efforts to deter, prevent, and defeat cyber incidents across all CIKR sectors.

Federal Bureau of Investigation (FBI)

The FBI:

- Maintains awareness of critical DIB assets;
- Ensures that the respective critical DIB asset owner/operator receives at least one face-to-face contact annually with the assigned Special Agent in Charge;
- Investigates reported suspicious activity and provides feedback to the reporting official; and
- Responds to incidents as required by the asset owner/operator or State and local law-enforcement officials.

Department of Energy (DOE)

The DOE National Nuclear Security Administration (NNSA) enhances national security through military application of nuclear energy, and by reducing the global threat from terrorism and weapons of mass destruction.

Department of Commerce (DOC)

The DOC Bureau of Industry and Security (BIS) advances national security, foreign policy, and economic objectives by enforcing an effective export control and treaty compliance system and promoting continued U.S. strategic technology security and DIB leadership. BIS administers the DPAS regulation (title 15, Code of Federal Regulations (CFR) Part 700) to require preferential acceptance and performance of contracts and orders for materials, services, and facilities needed to support approved national defense programs, including CIP and restoration. BIS also conducts primary research and analysis of critical technologies and industrial capabilities of key defense-related sectors using detailed surveys to provide essential financial and production data. The Defense Production Act of 1950, as amended, and Executive Order 12656 authorize these activities.

The DOC National Telecommunications and Information Administration carries out the primary mission-essential function to "achieve robust communications capability for the Industrial/ Commercial Sector," directly supporting national essential functions and the DOC role relating to the economic security component of CIP and homeland security. In addition, DOC CIP responsibilities ensure that the U.S. commercial and industrial sectors acquire diverse communications capabilities.

The DOC NIST, through its Manufacturing Extension Partnership, offers technical and business assistance to smaller DIB manufacturers.

Department of the Treasury (DOT)

The Secretary of the Treasury chairs the Committee on Foreign Investment in the United States (CFIUS). DoD and 11 other Federal departments and agencies participate in CFIUS to advise the President on exercising his authority to suspend or prohibit a foreign acquisition, merger, or takeover of a U.S. corporation that would threaten U.S. national security.

Department of State (DOS)

- Supports the efforts of DoD, foreign nations, and international organizations to strengthen- protection of critical DIB assets located outside the United States;

- Facilitates exchange of information between host nations, overseas DIB critical asset owners, and DoD;

- Supports the U.S. ability to safeguard national security and further foreign policy objectives by controlling the export and temporary import of defense articles and services covered by the United States Munitions List.

White House Office of Science and Technology Policy (OSTP)

OSTP coordinates interagency R&D to enhance protection of critical infrastructure, helps to identify research requirements and technologies that are applicable to the DIB, and shares information on those technologies with DoD and the DIB.

State and Local Agencies

DoD conducts outreach to State and local authorities to coordinate the government role for protection of the DIB. This relationship ensures incorporation of critical DIB assets and their supporting infrastructure (e.g., telecommunications, road or rail, energy, cyber networks) into local law enforcement and other emergency response planning. Emergency plans will address prioritization of response and restoration of services; the level of resources required to meet emergency needs; monitoring of the assets under their cognizance in the local environment; and advice, assistance, and warning of impending threats and hazards.

International Organizations and Foreign Countries

DoD works with other Federal departments and agencies, foreign governments, and international organizations to address critical DIB CIKR assets that are located outside the United States. DoD is developing an international strategy to improve protection and resilience of DIB assets and ensure continued availability of critical assets outside the United States. DoD seeks to leverage the expertise of international partners to improve its own capabilities in counterterrorism, maritime interception, and other missions critical to an active, layered defense. Key partnerships include:

North American Technology Industrial Base Organization (NATIBO)

DoD and the Canadian DND chartered NATIBO in 1987. NATIBO's primary purpose is to identify and analyze key industrial sectors that are critical to defense, assess the viability of these sectors, identify issues and barriers related to viability, and develop strategies to enhance and sustain the health of the marketplace. NATIBO is committed to coordinating North American technology industrial base activities by promoting a cost-effective and healthy technology industrial base that is responsive to the national and economic security needs of the United States and Canada. The goals of the partnership are to:

- Improve the defense posture of the North American technology and industrial base;

- Reduce redundant efforts through bilateral cooperation on studies and projects relating to the defense technology and industrial base of the United States and Canada; and

- Ensure the United States and Canada take into account North American technology and industrial base considerations during military and/or civilian emergency planning.

DND-Canada

The role of DND is to:

- Work through a DoD/DND Steering Committee and Working Group to assist the two countries in obtaining a comprehensive DIB awareness, thereby providing a framework to enhance bilateral security and obtain mission assurance;

- Assist in strategizing the establishment of a Canadian Defense Industrial Base Program to include critical infrastructure similar to the ASD (HD&ASA) DCIP;

- Collaborate on a common CAL; and

- Define requirements for a bi-national protection program.

Security and Prosperity Partnership (SPP) for North America

The governments of the United States, Canada, and Mexico are launching the next generation of their common security strategy to further secure North America and ensure the streamlined movement of legitimate travelers and cargo across our shared borders. To this end, the three governments will work together to ensure the highest continent-wide security standards and streamlined, risk-based border processes are achieved.